HBCU SPORTS 101

A GUIDE TO UNDERSTANDING BLACK COLLEGE ATHLETICS

KENN RASHAD

HBCU Sports 101: A Guide to Understanding Black College Athletics

Published by Rashad Media

Paperback ISBN: 979-8-9988656-0-2

Paperback ISBN: 979-8-9988656-4-0

Hardcover ISBN: 979-8-9988656-1-9

E-book ISBN: 979-8-9988656-2-6

Audiobook ISBN: 979-8-9988656-3-3

Printed in the United States of America

"And when he had taken the five loaves and the two fishes, he looked up to heaven, and blessed, and brake the loaves, and gave them to his disciples to set before them; and the two fishes divided he among them all.

And they did all eat, and were filled."

— MARK 6:41–42

DEDICATION

To the One who made everything out of nothing
I dedicate this book to God. For the vision, the voice, and the calling to tell these stories. Without His grace, none of this exists.

To the ones who made something out of nothing
This is for every builder, dreamer, and believer who helped shape the HBCU experience. Your ability to do more with less is the foundation this culture stands on.

To those still carrying the torch
You remind us that God can stretch what little we have and make it sacred.

And to the town of Grambling, Louisiana, where my HBCU roots were planted
Thank you to my great-grandfather, my grandparents, my mother, my brother, my aunts, uncles, cousins, and the community friends who poured into me. You exposed me to a culture that shaped my calling in ways I'm still uncovering.
This book exists because of you. And I pray it honors the legacy we share.

CONTENTS

INTRODUCTION

Long before I became a student at Grambling State University, a journalist, or the founder of a media platform, I had a front-row seat to the HBCU experience.

Growing up between Inglewood, California, and Grambling, Louisiana, I didn't just discover this world in college; I was immersed in it throughout my childhood. Twice, I lived with my grandparents in Grambling, once as a first grader and again during my seventh and eighth-grade years. While others would later discover the HBCU experience as actual college students, I lived it before I ever filled out an application.

I didn't just know the names that helped shape the HBCU sports landscape; I knew the people. Coach Eddie Robinson? I didn't learn about him from books or documentaries. I hung out at his house. His grandchildren were, and still are, my friends to this very day. Coach Fred Hobdy, who built Grambling basketball into a powerhouse, was a familiar face in the community. Ralph Waldo Emerson "Prez" Jones, the former university president and baseball coach, would often wave to me from the stands at baseball games, calling me over to sit with him and the team in the dugout. Prez knew my grandparents. He was a family friend.

But it wasn't just the coaches or community leaders who shaped my connection to Grambling. It was that familiar sound.

Every day during football season, I could hear the World Famed Tiger Marching Band practicing from my grandparents' house. The band hall was less than a mile away, and when the beating of the drums started, the whole town knew. You didn't need a ticket or a seat in the stands to feel the vibe. The band's soundtrack came to you.

I remember standing outside on the porch of my grandparents' house, just listening. The brass section was sharp and loud, the drum beats carried through the trees, and you could feel the energy of a halftime show slowly taking shape. Sometimes I'd walk onto campus just to watch them practice. To a kid from the Los Angeles suburb of Inglewood, living in this small Louisiana town, it felt like magic. And it stuck with me.

The band made such an impression that when I returned to Inglewood for high school, I joined the Inglewood High School marching band. But it didn't end there. As fate would have it, my high school band director was none other than Conrad Hutchinson III, the son of the legendary Conrad Hutchinson Jr., who had led the very same World Famed Tiger Marching Band I grew up listening to. That kind of full-circle moment doesn't just happen. It was another reminder that Grambling wasn't just in my past—it was in my path.

Even before high school, when I was in middle school during those seventh and eighth-grade years in Grambling, I marched in the band. The school was small, so the middle and high schoolers played in the same ensemble.

(And in case you're wondering, I played the trumpet.)

That kind of early exposure—hearing the music, feeling the pride, and seeing the discipline up close and in person stuck with me. I wasn't just watching HBCU culture unfold around me. I was part of it, even before I fully understood it.

It's just one more example of how deeply rooted the HBCU experience is in my life. I didn't just grow up around Grambling during parts of my life; parts of my life were shaped by it: the band, the football team, the community, the traditions. So by the time I got to college, I hadn't discovered HBCU culture because I had already lived it.

My Grambling connection runs deeper than childhood memories. My great-grandfather worked as a night watchman on campus. Both of my grandparents spent their careers working for the university. My mother, a Grambling native, graduated from the local high school and later enrolled at the university. Today, my son carries the legacy forward as a Grambling graduate. I come from a long line of aunts, uncles, and cousins who've all called that campus home. Grambling isn't just my alma mater. It's part of my inheritance. It's a thread in the fabric my family's been stitching for generations.

One of the most memorable Grambling football games I attended was in 1980. It was my second time living in Grambling as a seventh grader. The game was played in Shreveport, Louisiana, at Independence Stadium—about an hour down I-20 from Grambling. The contest was then known as the Red River Classic, an early-season matchup that always drew a crowd. That year, Grambling was facing off against a powerhouse Alcorn State team led by the legendary Marino Casem.

Our family made the trip in two cars, caravanning down the interstate with my aunts, uncles, and cousins. I remember seeing car after car with Mississippi license plates, packed with Alcorn fans. As we passed each other, people waved their purple and gold shakers in the air. And we waved our black and gold ones right back. It was all part of the show. Even on the road, the rivalry was real.

When we arrived in Shreveport, the atmosphere felt bigger

than football. The stadium was packed. Black folks filled every section, shoulder to shoulder, with nothing but school pride and anticipation. For a kid seeing it all in person for the first time, it was overwhelming in the best way. Everyone talked about Coach Eddie Robinson and the Grambling Tigers football team for weeks leading up to the game. And now, I was finally watching them live.

The game itself was a battle. Grambling lost to Alcorn State 29–27 in a tight contest, but that 1980 Grambling squad would go on to become SWAC champions and eventually face Boise State in the first round of the NCAA I-AA playoffs. But as memorable as the game was, it was the moments off the football field that stuck with me most.

I'll never forget what happened before kickoff, while one of the bands played the Star-Spangled Banner. They had reached the song's final line "…and the home of the—." Before the word *brave* could land, the entire Alcorn crowd roared in unison:

"Braves!"

It caught me off guard. I had never seen anything like that before. It wasn't just clever. It was cultural identity in full voice. It was dope!

As I later learned, that reaction to the national anthem by Alcorn fans wasn't just an isolated moment. It's a tradition that Alcorn fans continue to this day.

After the final whistle, something else stood out. As fans poured out of the stadium and into the parking lots, you could see Grambling and Alcorn supporters—people who had been on opposite sides of the field just minutes earlier—talking, laughing, and wishing each other a safe trip home. That was the beauty of it. The rivalry was real, but so was the respect.

That night didn't just introduce me to the Red River Classic featuring two powerhouse HBCU football teams. It introduced me to the full experience of HBCU sports culture, community, tradition, pride, and unity all wrapped up in one unforgettable day.

Living in Grambling meant that campus life, community pride, and HBCU culture weren't separate things. They were all part of daily life. So, when I enrolled at Grambling State, I wasn't stepping into a new world. I was stepping deeper into the cultural roots that had helped raise me.

As a student journalist, I covered athletes and moments that were shaping HBCU history in real time. I covered NFL-bound athletes like Jake Reed, Fred Jones, and Andrew Glover. I watched Fred McNair (Steve McNair's older brother) and Cedric "C.C." Tillman shine at Alcorn State. I witnessed Jackson State's Lewis Tillman break Walter Payton's all-time rushing record. I saw a young Aeneas Williams, who would eventually be inducted into the Pro Football Hall of Fame, take the field for Southern University. I watched Patricia Hoskins dominate NCAA stat sheets in points and rebounds for Mississippi Valley State women's basketball. I sat courtside in Grambling's Men's Memorial Gymnasium during the golden era of Ben Jobe's Southern basketball teams when Bobby Phills and Avery Johnson were lighting up the SWAC.

Eventually, I realized these moments weren't just games. They were living proof that greatness was already growing on HBCU campuses, whether the rest of the world noticed or not. But the reality was that most of the world wasn't paying attention. Coverage was thin. Recognition was rare. HBCU sports were often an afterthought, if they were thought of at all. At some point, I just accepted the truth: if these stories were going to be told, I was the one who had to do it.

In 1997, frustrated by the lack of consistent coverage, I launched a basic website called *The SWAC Page*. It wasn't a business plan, a brand strategy, or anything else. It was just me figuring out how to post scores and recaps using a few megabytes of server space, a dial-up connection offered by my local phone company, and a book on HTML I picked up from a local CompUSA.

At first, I updated it out of curiosity. Nothing more. But keeping the site updated was time-consuming, and after a few weeks, I stopped. I figured no one cared enough to notice.

Then, the emails started.

People were asking for scores, recaps, and updates. I realized then that the demand for HBCU sports coverage was real. It wasn't loud, but it was loyal, and it deserved better than what it had been getting.

Over time, that small project eventually became *HBCU Sports* (hbcusports.com), one of the first digital platforms fully dedicated to covering Black college athletics.

And we didn't just post scores.

We started by curating press releases from sports information directors at HBCUs across the country. Then, we launched a fan message board. It became a hub for passionate fans from different SWAC and other HBCU schools to connect, debate, talk a little trash, and build community. That message board got so popular that we eventually started organizing in-person meetups every summer in places like Atlanta, Jackson, New Orleans, and Houston.

As our audience grew, so did our ambitions. We began producing original content. Before long, we weren't just sharing news—we were breaking it. That's when *HBCU Sports* shifted from being a fan space to a respected national media platform.

Fast forward to 2020, Jackson State University was preparing to hire Deion Sanders as its head football coach. This move would send shockwaves through college football and elevate the JSU athletic program into a new era of visibility. While mainstream outlets later caught wind of the decision, *HBCU Sports* broke the story, not because of speculation, but because we were deeply connected to the people, the culture, and the institutions shaping these moments.

This book traces a journey deeper than games and statistics. It's about institutions that created their own paths when traditional routes were closed to them. It's about athletes who transformed their sports but waited decades for proper recognition. It's about coaches who built winning teams and developed complete individuals. It's about a culture that never waited for permission to achieve excellence. My path from that basic website with a dial-up connection to breaking national stories like Deion Sanders joining Jackson State mirrors the HBCU experience—creating something meaningful from limited resources and eventually commanding the attention it deserves.

WHY THIS BOOK MATTERS

This book isn't a nostalgia trip. It's not a highlight reel. It's not about begging for mainstream attention.

It's about telling the real story, how it deserves to be told.

HBCUs didn't wait for inclusion. They built their own stages. They created their own lanes when the doors were locked. They made history whether anyone else was ready to acknowledge it or not.

This book doesn't shy away from the challenges. It faces them head-on. It's about what was built, what was lost, what was fought for, and what still needs fighting for today.

The culture has always been bigger than the headlines. It's time the story matched it.

WHO THIS BOOK IS FOR

This book is for high school students wondering if an HBCU is the right fit, for alums who still feel something stirring when the band plays the fight song, for fans who never miss a game, for educators shaping young minds, and yes, even for corporate partners trying to make an authentic connection with this culture.

If you believe that history still matters and that the legacies built through struggle, excellence, and community are worth protecting, this book is for you.

The HBCU story has always been ours to tell.

So, let's tell it.

What follows is both historical documentation and a blueprint, showing how HBCUs established athletic programs that produced excellence despite systematic barriers. We'll examine the founding institutions that laid the groundwork, profile the players who redefined their sports, honor the coaches who built dynasties with a fraction of the resources, analyze the conference structures that shaped competition, celebrate the traditions that built community wealth, trace how HBCU talent transformed professional sports, and confront the real challenges that will determine the future. Throughout, we're not just documenting what happened—we're demonstrating why it matters not just to HBCU communities, but to American sports culture as a whole.

ONE
WHAT IS AN HBCU?

B efore understanding the power of HBCU athletics, we must understand the world that shaped it. And that begins by understanding what an HBCU is and what it represents.

An HBCU isn't just a college. It's a declaration. It's a refusal to accept invisibility. It's where we can be seen, heard, and celebrated on our terms. It's where Black excellence was (and still is) cultivated, celebrated, and launched into a world that wasn't designed to accommodate it. When most people hear the term "HBCU," they often think it's just a category on a college list. But it's so much more than that.

BUILT FROM THE GROUND UP

Historically Black Colleges and Universities (HBCUs) are institutions of higher learning established before 1964 with the principal mission of educating Black Americans, a designation formally defined in the Higher Education Act of 1965. They were born out of necessity—a direct response to the exclusionary practices of predominantly white institutions (PWIs), which for generations barred Black students from admission simply because of their race.

The first HBCUs emerged in the early 19th century before the Civil War ended. Institutions like Cheyney University, founded in 1837, and Lincoln University in 1854, laid the groundwork. Access to education was not something Black communities would wait for. It was something they would build themselves.

Over time, the number of HBCUs grew dramatically, especially during Reconstruction and the following decades. They became anchors of Black advancement, producing generations of teachers, doctors, engineers, activists, artists, and athletes.

But HBCUs weren't just places of academic rigor. They were cultural sanctuaries, breeding grounds for leadership, innovation, and resistance. These schools weren't built on trust funds or endowments. They were built on grit, sacrifice, and the unshakable belief that Black futures mattered.

When we talk about HBCUs, we are talking about institutions that did more than teach coursework. They taught survival. They taught excellence. They taught pride.

While predominantly white institutions evolved with generational wealth and public investment, HBCUs fought for scraps, while still managing to produce towering figures who would shape every facet of American society.

That spirit wasn't just limited to classrooms or lecture halls. It found its way onto athletic fields, basketball courts, and running tracks. But even before sports entered the picture, there was something distinct about everyday life on an HBCU campus.

CULTURE BEYOND THE CLASSROOM

At an HBCU, traditions aren't just part of the experience; they are the experience. And nothing captures that better than homecoming.

At most colleges, homecoming means a football game and a few alumni events scattered across campus. At an HBCU, homecoming hits differently.

It's not a weekend. It's a takeover. A week-long celebration that turns the campus into something electric. Alumni fly in from every direction. Classes still happen, technically, but most people are somewhere between the yard and the tailgate. The band is out, sometimes leading the parade that kicks off the weekend, turning the streets into a moving concert. So are the food trucks, the BBQ pits, and the vendors selling Greek gear and "HBCU Made" tees.

And while the football game is technically the headline, it's not always the main draw. For some folks, the tailgate *is* the show. The grills are hot by noon. DJs are blending R&B, southern soul, blues, and hip hop music like it's one seamless playlist. Aunties two-stepping. Old heads debating. Everybody's got a plate in one hand and a drink in the other.

But it's more than a party. It's a reunion across generations. You'll see toddlers in tiny cheerleading outfits. Teenagers are already talking about which dorm they want to stay in. Grandparents who marched in the band back in '72. A freshman and a 30-year alum might dap each other up like they're family— because in many ways, they are.

That's what makes HBCU homecoming different. It's not just a return to campus. It's a return to identity.

But homecoming is just one part of it.

You can't talk about HBCU culture without talking about Greek life, specifically, the Divine Nine, or D9. These historically Black fraternities and sororities include Alpha Phi Alpha, Alpha Kappa Alpha, Kappa Alpha Psi, Omega Psi Phi, Delta Sigma Theta, Phi Beta Sigma, Zeta Phi Beta, Sigma Gamma Rho, and Iota Phi Theta. These aren't just social organizations. They're rooted in service, legacy, and leadership. On most campuses, the presence of Black Greek-letter organizations is felt daily, whether through strolls on the yard, a scholarship fundraiser, a community project, or a probate show that packs the entire basketball arena, auditorium, or student union.

At HBCUs, pledging a fraternity or sorority is bigger than letters. It's about history. It's about family. It's about becoming part of something that existed long before you, and will still be going long after graduation. And for me, that's not theory—it's personal. I'm a member of Kappa Alpha Psi Fraternity, Inc. My wife is a member of Alpha Kappa Alpha Sorority, Inc. My son is also a Kappa, and my sister-in-laws are members of Delta Sigma Theta Sorority, Inc. For us, Greek life isn't just a tradition. It's a part of our identity. And when you're on an HBCU campus, it doesn't matter if you're a freshman or a fifty-year-old alum— those letters still carry weight.

Each organization has its own identity, chants, colors, and traditions. But collectively, the Divine Nine shape the rhythm of campus life. They set the tone, run student government, lead service initiatives, and organize the social calendar. And when is it time to represent? They show up and show out.

Step shows aren't just performances. They're statements, fusing rhythm, athleticism, and legacy into something you feel in your chest before the first stomp even hits. But Greek life at an HBCU isn't defined by step shows alone. It's also the bond. The mentorship. The accountability. The idea that someone's got your back, because you're not just a student. You're family.

While I can't speak to the Greek life experience at PWIs firsthand, I know that at HBCUs, Greek life is deeply woven into the fabric of campus life, seen in everything from campus leadership to cultural expression. It's not just about socializing. It's about showing up for your people, your school, and your community.

THE UNIQUE BOND ACROSS HBCUS

While we often discuss the culture of HBCUs broadly, it's essential to understand that no two campuses are precisely the same. Each HBCU has its unique traditions, customs, and identity. The vibe at Delaware State isn't the same as that at Central State, and Bowie State moves differently from Virginia Union. From student leadership to homecoming rituals, every campus has its unique flavor.

But something else ties them all together, a kind of unspoken kinship among those who've lived the HBCU experience. You can see it when alumni from different schools meet for the first time. There's an immediate connection, a mutual respect. We may talk trash to each other during football season. We may argue about who has the best band, the best yard, the best legacy, etc. But let something happen to one of our institutions, whether it's public disrespect from a mainstream outlet, a funding crisis, or a campus emergency, and suddenly those rivalries dissolve into solidarity.

In that sense, the HBCU community operates like a cultural alliance. Call it what you want—fellowship, family, or even our own version of NATO. The message is the same: an attack on one is felt by all of us. That's why you'll see a Howard grad going to bat for someone who attended Prairie View. Or a Grambling alum donating to Benedict College during a fundraising campaign. It's why a stranger wearing an HBCU hoodie, who sees you wearing one, can nod to you in an airport, and it means something. That kind of connection can't be manufactured. It's lived. And it's deeply understood among those of us who've been part of it.

PURPOSE BEFORE POWERHOUSES

Today, HBCUs continue to serve a critical role. They represent about 3% of the nation's colleges and universities but produce nearly 20% of all African American graduates. They cultivate leadership, innovation, and resilience—the same spirit that has fueled their athletic traditions for over a century. And while media coverage often comes and goes based on trends or headlines, the power of HBCUs has never been about visibility alone. It has been about purpose and permanence.

HBCUs weren't created with the goal of building powerhouse athletic programs. They were built to educate, empower, and uplift. But over time, powerhouse programs became a byproduct of that mission. When HBCUs first fielded teams, they weren't merely participating in sports but making powerful statements about capability and excellence. At a time when mainstream sports pages ignored Black athletes entirely, HBCUs built athletic departments that showcased Black talent on their terms. They didn't wait for invitations to join existing competitions. Instead, they created their own standards and traditions. Sports became more than recreation. They became expressions of resistance, community pride, and cultural affirmation. What began as a necessity evolved into the traditions, rivalries, and legacies that would eventually produce talent so undeniable that the professional leagues and Olympic committees could no longer maintain their exclusionary practices. The NFL, NBA, MLB, and Olympic podiums would subsequently make space for athletes who developed their skills on HBCU fields and courts.

WHERE THE STORY BEGINS

Understanding what an HBCU is means understanding what happens when excellence refuses to be denied. When the doors were locked, Black America didn't just petition for entry. It built its own house and then filled that house with unmistakable greatness.

The story of HBCU athletics begins here, in these institutions built through sacrifice, sustained through struggle, and defined by an uncompromising belief in Black potential. These weren't simply schools that happened to have sports teams. They were communities where every touchdown, every fast break, every home run became evidence that the talent was always present, even when the spotlight wasn't. What followed wasn't just athletic competition; it was a movement that would produce some of the most transformative athletes and coaches in history. Names that wouldn't just enter record books but would fundamentally change their sports.

Now that you understand what HBCUs are, it's time to explore how they used athletics not just for competition, but as a platform to demand space, command respect, and build community in a world that never intended to give them either.

TWO
A BRIEF HISTORY OF BLACK COLLEGE ATHLETICS

T he story of HBCU athletics isn't just about wins, losses, or trophies. It's about access, pride, and carving out a space where excellence could thrive, even when the system was built to keep Black athletes on the outside looking in.

Black college football traces its roots back to December 27, 1892, when Livingstone College and Biddle University (now Johnson C. Smith University) met on the snowy grounds of Livingstone's campus in Salisbury, North Carolina. That game, widely recognized as the first football contest between two HBCUs, was more than a match. It was a statement of intent. At a time when Black institutions were shut out of organized collegiate athletics, these two schools created their own path, setting the stage for generations of competition, camaraderie, and cultural pride.

But even before that snowy December day, another sport had already begun planting roots. In 1887, five years before that first football game, Southern University and Straight University (now Dillard University) played the first documented intercollegiate baseball game between Black colleges. The game was played in New Orleans, where both schools were based at the time.

Although the score and finer details have been lost to history, the meaning of the moment is still clear.

It wasn't just about baseball. It was about showing what could be built when the opportunity wasn't given. These early contests weren't part of any official league or conference, but they carried the weight of something bigger. They showed how Black colleges turned exclusion into motivation, creating athletic traditions centered on excellence and belonging.

From those early steps in baseball and football, HBCUs began developing athletic cultures that went beyond the scoreboard. Sports became a way to strengthen community, instill discipline, and showcase the talent that others refused to see. And even in the absence of media attention or institutional support, the foundation had already been laid.

BUILT TO COMPETE

In the early 20th century, when segregation barred Black athletes from competing at predominantly white institutions, HBCUs developed their own athletic systems. These weren't second-rate substitutes. They were carefully organized, competitive structures built to serve Black student-athletes and their communities.

The Colored Intercollegiate Athletic Association, founded in 1912 and later renamed the Central Intercollegiate Athletic Association (CIAA), was the first formal conference. Its founding members included:

- Hampton Institute (now Hampton University)
- Howard University
- Lincoln University of Pennsylvania
- Shaw University
- Virginia Union University

The Southern Intercollegiate Athletic Conference (SIAC) followed in 1913. Its founding members included:

- Alabama State University
- Atlanta University (now Clark Atlanta University)
- Clark College (now Clark Atlanta University)
- Fisk University
- Jackson College (now Jackson State University)
- Morris Brown College
- Morehouse College
- Talladega College
- Tuskegee Institute (now Tuskegee University)

The Southwestern Athletic Conference (SWAC), founded in 1920, launched with:

- Bishop College
- Paul Quinn College
- Prairie View A&M
- Texas College
- Wiley College (now Wiley University)

These weren't just administrative leagues. They were acts of agency during a time of forced exclusion.

In 1970, the Mid-Eastern Athletic Conference (MEAC) separated from the CIAA to establish a Division I presence on the East Coast. Its charter members included:

- Delaware State
- Howard University
- University of Maryland Eastern Shore
- Morgan State
- North Carolina A&T
- North Carolina Central

- South Carolina State

In 2024, the Gulf Coast Athletic Conference formally rebranded as the HBCU Athletic Conference (HBCUAC), cementing its identity as an NAIA home for Black institutions.

"This question around who we are and where do we want to be—we had to answer that first before we could move forward," HBCUAC Commissioner Dr. Kiki Baker Barnes said to me during an interview on the *HBCU Sports Podcast*. "We've been this group of HBCUs that have continued to win over and over again, but people might not necessarily know us as a collective. Now it's time for everyone to know who we are. For me personally, I want to own the search engines. Every time you put 'HBCU' and 'athletic' in, once we get rolling, we're going to show up."

While smaller than the NCAA, the NAIA has long served as a home for many HBCUs, offering scholarship opportunities and national competition outside the traditional Division I spotlight. In fact, several of today's NCAA-affiliated HBCUs began their athletic journeys in the NAIA before transitioning to the NCAA structure.

These conference transformations were more than strategic; they were declarations of visibility and self-determination. And while each shared a mission to uplift Black athletes, they also developed distinct identities rooted in their regions and traditions.

The CIAA became synonymous with Black college basketball, home to one of the most celebrated tournaments in the nation. The SIAC helped define Southern Black football culture. The SWAC became a cultural giant in the Deep South, blending elite football with iconic marching band traditions. The MEAC gave HBCUs a platform to compete on a national Division I stage. And now, the HBCUAC is writing its own chapter—one rooted in reinvention, identity, and purpose.

Since the system wouldn't make space for Black excellence, HBCUs built their own spaces. In the next chapter, we'll examine how those conferences operate today and why their structure still matters.

EXCELLENCE AGAINST THE ODDS

Even without national rankings or the resources other schools had, HBCUs didn't just show up; they proved they belonged. They produced Olympians, pro athletes, and powerhouse programs built on determination, vision, and the pride of their communities.

At Tennessee State, legendary track and field coach Ed Temple led the Tigerbelles to international dominance, producing 40 Olympians and 23 Olympic medalists. Florida A&M rose to national prominence in football under Coach Jake Gaither. And at Grambling State, Coach Eddie Robinson built a football dynasty that sent over 200 players to the NFL, more than many top-tier programs at predominantly white institutions.

But the excellence didn't stop there. HBCUs have produced legends in nearly every sport. Southern University's Rickie Weeks became the No. 2 overall pick in the 2003 MLB Draft. Winston-Salem State's Earl "The Pearl" Monroe redefined basketball long before his NBA stardom.

Across the board, HBCU coaches weren't just building teams —they were building systems. Leaders like Gaither, Robinson, and Temple didn't just teach strategy; they cultivated discipline, leadership, and pride with minimal resources and maximum impact.

And it wasn't just about the players and coaches. HBCUs filled stadiums, often with no media spotlight in sight. Local communities packed the stands, supported the programs, and turned game day into a cultural event. These institutions didn't wait for national coverage to validate them. They built traditions and excellence on their own terms.

LEGACY TEAMS THAT CHANGED THE GAME

The story of HBCU athletics isn't just about standout athletes. Some of the most potent statements were made by teams that, through unity, execution, and culture, shattered expectations and redefined what Black excellence could look like on the field, court, or track. These weren't one-off upsets. They were eras. They were movements.

- **Grambling State (Football, 1942)** – Eddie Robinson led the Tigers to a perfect 9–0 season in just his second year as head coach. They finished undefeated, untied, and unscored upon—one of the rarest feats in college football history. It was a powerful statement during an era when HBCUs were shut out of national competition. *(At the time, the school was known as Louisiana Negro Normal and Industrial Institute.)*

- **Tennessee A&I (Men's Basketball, 1957–59)** – Under Coach John McLendon, the Tigers became the first college basketball team at any level to win three consecutive national championships. In an era when few Black coaches were recognized, McLendon's team made history impossible to ignore. *(Now known as Tennessee State University.)*

- **Tennessee State – The Tigerbelles (Track & Field, 1956–1984)** – With Ed Temple at the helm, the Tigerbelles didn't just dominate in track and field. They redefined it. Producing more than 40 Olympians and 23 medals, the program became a global model for what disciplined, intentional coaching could produce, even without the budgets of larger schools.

- **Winston-Salem State (Men's Basketball, 1967)** – Coach Clarence "Big House" Gaines and Earl "The Pearl" Monroe led the Rams to an NCAA Division II title—the first for any HBCU. Monroe's scoring brilliance captured national attention, but the win also cemented Gaines as one of the greatest minds in the game.

- **Florida A&M (Football, 1978)** – The Rattlers, under Coach Rudy Hubbard, won the NCAA Division I-AA national title (still the only HBCU to do so). They didn't just win a trophy; they proved that an HBCU could run the table when finally given access to the same playoff system as everyone else.

- **Cheyney State (Women's Basketball, 1982)** – Coach Vivian Stringer led the Lady Wolves to the NCAA Division I Women's Final Four. Still unmatched by any HBCU men's or women's program, that feat put Black women's coaching brilliance on the national stage.

EXCELLENCE IGNORED

Even as HBCUs broke records and filled stadiums, national media coverage remained inconsistent at best. Mainstream outlets often overlooked achievements that would have been front-page news elsewhere. That neglect wasn't incidental. It was systemic.

HBCUs had to fund their own programs, promote their own athletes, and celebrate their own victories. And Black-owned newspapers—those community-rooted outlets—kept the receipts. Publications like the *Pittsburgh Courier*, *Chicago Defender*, and *Baltimore Afro-American* didn't just cover the games; they told the whole story. They highlighted athletes who were ignored by the wire services. They profiled coaches who built dynasties without budgets. They held space for Black excellence when no one else would. Without them, much of HBCU sports history might never have been documented.

They made sure the excellence wasn't erased. They told the truth when no one else would. And they weren't alone in that effort. While few outside of Black communities were paying attention, people like Collie J. Nicholson took it upon themselves to make sure the stories were told. Nicholson, who served as Grambling State's first sports information director from 1948 to 1978, helped put HBCU athletics on the national map. He arranged games at Yankee Stadium, helped create the Bayou Classic, and brought national and even international attention to the program by securing games in Tokyo and media coverage that would've otherwise never come. He showed what it looked like to shape the narrative from the inside. Doing so helped redefine how HBCU athletics were seen across the country.

Because of work like his and the coverage sustained by the Black press, the rivalries, classics, and cultural milestones built at HBCUs didn't just survive. They became sacred inside Black communities, even if they went unacknowledged everywhere else.

THE IMPACT OF INTEGRATION

The civil rights movement and the integration of college athletics in the 1960s and '70s changed the playing field. PWIs, now eager to win, began recruiting Black athletes en masse. HBCUs lost access to top talent, and with it came a slow decline in national visibility and media attention.

TV contracts, donor money, and national rankings followed the talent. HBCUs, once the epicenter of Black athletic achievement, had to fight to remain relevant in a system they helped build.

And while integration opened long-overdue doors for individual athletes, it came at a cost. HBCUs lost not only their stars, but also the attention, revenue, and recognition that came with them. Black coaches who had built powerhouse programs were rarely given the same opportunities at newly integrated institutions. The schools that once carried the weight of Black college sports were suddenly expected to cheer from the sidelines of a game they helped invent.

WHEN THE SPOTLIGHT RETURNED

In 2020, a national reckoning on race, sparked by the murder of George Floyd, brought HBCUs back into focus. Five-star basketball recruit Makur Maker shocked the college basketball world by committing to Howard University. Around the same time, twin volleyball standouts Mikayla and Mariah Allison made headlines when they decommitted from Texas A&M and chose to play at Howard instead, making a bold statement about identity, representation, and belonging. Shortly after, Jackson State hired Deion Sanders as head football coach.

Suddenly, HBCU athletics—especially at Jackson State—returned to the national conversation. Corporate sponsors took interest, and media platforms scrambled to catch up. But when Sanders left Jackson State for Colorado, the media spotlight followed him, not the movement. For a brief moment, it felt like HBCUs might finally get the recognition they'd long deserved. But his departure made it clear: the spotlight had been focused on him, not the institutions, not the athletes, and not the culture that made the moment possible in the first place.

A LEGACY STILL IN MOTION

The history of HBCU athletics is layered and unfinished. It's a story of building from the ground up, of daring to compete without permission. It's a story of athletes, coaches, and programs that showed up not just to play, but to prove something bigger.

This isn't nostalgia. This is a living legacy, and it's still unfolding.

THREE

HBCU ATHLETIC CONFERENCES, DIVISIONS, AND IDENTITY

To understand HBCU athletics, you must understand its structure, which means understanding the conferences.

HBCU conferences aren't just about who plays who. They've shaped rivalries, stirred up school pride, pumped money into communities, and laid the foundation for how Black college sports have been built and recognized for over a century. They've held the culture together when nothing else did.

Five major conferences define the HBCU athletic landscape: the Southwestern Athletic Conference (SWAC), the Mid-Eastern Athletic Conference (MEAC), the Central Intercollegiate Athletic Association (CIAA), the Southern Intercollegiate Athletic Conference (SIAC), and most recently, the HBCU Athletic Conference (HBCUAC). Each one has its own history, identity, and role in the larger story.

Note: The following conference member schools are listed as of 2025, the year this book was published.

SOUTHWESTERN ATHLETIC CONFERENCE (SWAC)

Founded in 1920 in Houston, Texas, the SWAC is arguably the most recognizable HBCU athletic conference. Initially established by six member schools, its purpose was clear: to formalize competition and strengthen the visibility of Black college athletics in the Deep South. Today, the SWAC remains a powerhouse, home to some of the most celebrated programs and traditions in HBCU sports.

Current SWAC Member Institutions:

- **Alabama A&M University** – Normal, Alabama
- **Alabama State University** – Montgomery, Alabama
- **Alcorn State University** – Lorman, Mississippi
- **University of Arkansas at Pine Bluff (UAPB)** – Pine Bluff, Arkansas
- **Bethune–Cookman University** – Daytona Beach, Florida
- **Florida A&M University** – Tallahassee, Florida
- **Grambling State University** – Grambling, Louisiana
- **Jackson State University** – Jackson, Mississippi
- **Mississippi Valley State University** – Itta Bena, Mississippi
- **Prairie View A&M University** – Prairie View, Texas
- **Southern University** – Baton Rouge, Louisiana
- **Texas Southern University** – Houston, Texas

The SWAC's impact isn't just cultural. It has led the way in media visibility, securing major television contracts and producing some of the highest-profile athletes, coaches, and sports traditions in Black college athletics. The conference's geographic footprint expanded in 2021 when Florida A&M and Bethune-Cookman left the MEAC to become conference members.

MID-EASTERN ATHLETIC CONFERENCE (MEAC)

The MEAC was formed in 1970 when seven schools broke away from the CIAA to create a new Division I opportunity for HBCUs along the East Coast. Headquartered in Norfolk, Virginia, the MEAC has always been as much about academic excellence as athletic competition.

Current MEAC Member Institutions:

- **Coppin State University** – Baltimore, Maryland
- **Delaware State University** – Dover, Delaware
- **Howard University** – Washington, D.C.
- **Morgan State University** – Baltimore, Maryland
- **Norfolk State University** – Norfolk, Virginia
- **North Carolina Central University** – Durham, North Carolina
- **South Carolina State University** – Orangeburg, South Carolina
- **University of Maryland Eastern Shore (UMES)** – Princess Anne, Maryland

The MEAC is best known for producing champions in multiple sports and for its annual football clash with the SWAC in the Celebration Bowl, billed as the Black college football national championship. Despite challenges like realignment and shifting membership, the MEAC remains vital to the HBCU sports landscape.

CENTRAL INTERCOLLEGIATE ATHLETIC ASSOCIATION (CIAA)

The CIAA, founded in 1912, is the oldest HBCU athletic conference in the country. Originally known as the Colored Intercollegiate Athletic Association, it was created to organize athletic competition for Black colleges in the Mid-Atlantic region.

Current CIAA Member Institutions:

- **Bluefield State University** – Bluefield, West Virginia
- **Bowie State University** – Bowie, Maryland
- **Claflin University** – Orangeburg, South Carolina
- **Elizabeth City State University** – Elizabeth City, North Carolina
- **Fayetteville State University** – Fayetteville, North Carolina
- **Johnson C. Smith University** – Charlotte, North Carolina
- **Lincoln University (PA)** – Lincoln University, Pennsylvania
- **Livingstone College** – Salisbury, North Carolina
- **Saint Augustine's University** – Raleigh, North Carolina
- **Shaw University** – Raleigh, North Carolina
- **Virginia State University** – Petersburg, Virginia
- **Virginia Union University** – Richmond, Virginia
- **Winston-Salem State University** – Winston-Salem, North Carolina

The CIAA's impact stretches far beyond sports. Its annual CIAA Basketball Tournament is a cultural event that attracts fans, celebrities, and business leaders and generates millions in economic impact for host cities annually.

SOUTHERN INTERCOLLEGIATE ATHLETIC CONFERENCE (SIAC)

Formed in 1913, the SIAC was created to unite HBCUs in the Southeast for organized athletic competition. Based in Atlanta, Georgia, the SIAC places equal emphasis on athletic excellence and academic achievement, producing student-athletes who succeed both on the field and in the classroom.

Current SIAC Member Institutions:

- **Albany State University** – Albany, Georgia
- **Allen University** – Columbia, South Carolina
- **Benedict College** – Columbia, South Carolina
- **Central State University** – Wilberforce, Ohio
- **Clark Atlanta University** – Atlanta, Georgia
- **Edward Waters University** – Jacksonville, Florida
- **Fort Valley State University** – Fort Valley, Georgia
- **Kentucky State University** – Frankfort, Kentucky
- **Lane College** – Jackson, Tennessee
- **LeMoyne-Owen College** – Memphis, Tennessee
- **Miles College** – Fairfield, Alabama
- **Morehouse College** – Atlanta, Georgia
- **Savannah State University** – Savannah, Georgia
- **Spring Hill College** – Mobile, Alabama *(non-HBCU member)*
- **Tuskegee University** – Tuskegee, Alabama

Note: Spring Hill College is the only non-HBCU member in the SIAC.

The SIAC continues to serve as a critical space for developing athletic talent and preserving the culture and traditions that are foundational to HBCU life.

HBCU ATHLETIC CONFERENCE (HBCUAC)

The HBCUAC is the newest of the five, though its roots stretch back decades. Formerly known as the Gulf Coast Athletic Conference (GCAC), the conference officially rebranded in 2024 to reflect its all-HBCU membership.

Current HBCUAC Member Institutions:

- **Dillard University** – New Orleans, Louisiana
- **Fisk University** – Nashville, Tennessee
- **Oakwood University** – Huntsville, Alabama
- **Philander Smith University** – Little Rock, Arkansas
- **Rust College** – Holly Springs, Mississippi
- **Southern University at New Orleans** – New Orleans, Louisiana
- **Stillman College** – Tuscaloosa, Alabama
- **Talladega College** – Talladega, Alabama
- **Tougaloo College** – Tougaloo, Mississippi
- **University of the Virgin Islands (UVI)** – Charlotte Amalie, U.S. Virgin Islands
- **Voorhees University** – Denmark, South Carolina
- **Wilberforce University** – Wilberforce, Ohio
- **Wiley University** – Marshall, Texas
- **Huston-Tillotson University** – Austin, Texas
- **Paul Quinn College** – Dallas, Texas

Operating within the NAIA, the HBCUAC provides critical

opportunities for smaller Black colleges to compete at a high level while maintaining their cultural and historical identity.

NOT EVERY HBCU PLAYS IN AN HBCU CONFERENCE

While many HBCUs compete in the SWAC, MEAC, CIAA, SIAC, or the recently rebranded HBCUAC, not all historically Black colleges are part of historically Black conferences. Some compete in majority-White leagues across the NCAA, NAIA, or NJCAA levels due to regional, financial, or strategic reasons.

Tennessee State University, for example, has long been a member of the Ohio Valley Conference. Xavier University of Louisiana competes in the Red River Athletic Conference. Langston University plays in the Sooner Athletic Conference, and Harris-Stowe State University belongs to the American Midwest Conference.

In recent years, realignment has accelerated. Hampton University left the MEAC for the Big South Conference in 2018 and later moved to the Colonial Athletic Association in 2022. North Carolina A&T followed a similar path, leaving the MEAC in 2021 and eventually landing in the CAA as well. These transitions reflect broader trends in college athletics, driven by exposure, media rights, and postseason access. But they've also stirred debate about what HBCUs stand to gain or lose when stepping outside historically Black conferences. These aren't just strategic moves; they're cultural turning points.

Understanding where and why these shifts happen is key to understanding how modern HBCU athletics is shaped by tradition and change.

WHERE HBCUS COMPETE

To fully understand how HBCU conferences operate, it helps to know how they fit into the broader landscape of college athletics. HBCUs compete across several governing bodies, each with its own rules, budgets, and postseason systems:

- **NCAA Division I (FBS):** Often referred to as the "major" college football level, FBS includes programs like Alabama, Ohio State, and Georgia. These schools have the largest athletic budgets, national TV contracts, and access to the College Football Playoff. No HBCUs currently compete at the FBS level.

- **NCAA Division I (FCS):** A step below FBS, the FCS level features competitive football with smaller budgets and fewer scholarships, but still offers postseason play and national exposure. HBCUs in the Southwestern Athletic Conference (SWAC) and Mid-Eastern Athletic Conference (MEAC) compete here. These schools face high public expectations and steep financial demands compared to their FBS counterparts.

- **NCAA Division II:** Several HBCUs compete at the Division II level, particularly those in the Southern Intercollegiate Athletic Conference (SIAC) and Central Intercollegiate Athletic Association (CIAA). These programs offer athletic scholarships but typically operate with more limited budgets. They emphasize regional rivalries, community engagement, and access to NCAA playoffs in most sports.

- **NCAA Division III:** While no HBCUs currently compete at this level, Division III schools do not offer athletic scholarships. The emphasis is on academics, campus life, and the student-athlete experience, without the commercial pressures of higher divisions.

- **NAIA (National Association of Intercollegiate Athletics):** The NAIA allows more flexibility in scholarship distribution and often emphasizes return on investment for institutions. HBCUs affiliated with the **HBCU Athletic Conference (HBCUAC)** compete here, balancing athletic competition with missions grounded in education and access.

- **NJCAA (National Junior College Athletic Association):** Several two-year HBCUs compete in the NJCAA, which governs junior college athletics. These schools serve as key pipelines for student-athletes aiming to transfer to four-year programs. Examples include: Coahoma Community College (Mississippi), Shorter College (Arkansas) and Southern University at Shreveport (Louisiana).

HOW REVENUE GETS SHARED

It's one thing to understand who plays where. It's another to understand what that means financially. For HBCU athletic conferences, revenue distribution is not just about fairness—it's about survival.

Each conference has its own financial model, driven by a mix of media rights deals, sponsorships, NCAA or NAIA distributions, ticketed events, and donor contributions. But how that money gets distributed varies widely.

· · ·

SWAC: Leading the Pack in Revenue

Under Commissioner Dr. Charles McClelland, the SWAC has emerged as the most financially robust FCS conference in the country. A landmark media deal with HBCU Go, combined with ESPN coverage of premier events like the Celebration Bowl and the SWAC Championship Game, has generated over $28 million in revenue in just two years. While most revenue is shared among all 12 member institutions, some exceptions exist. For example, A member school retains profits when it hosts the SWAC Championship Football Game.

MEAC: Stability Through Annual Disbursements

The MEAC may not match the SWAC in total revenue, but it maintains consistent year-end payouts funded by NCAA tournament earnings, the Celebration Bowl, and corporate sponsorships. Schools are also rewarded for academic success with bonus distributions based on Graduation Success Rates and Academic Progress Rates. The conference also maintains media exposure through its tie-in with ESPN for the Celebration Bowl and has explored expanded media partnerships.

CIAA: Prioritizing Scholarships and Local Impact

The CIAA's biggest financial weapon is its basketball tournament, which draws tens of thousands to Baltimore annually and generates millions in economic impact. Most of its revenue is funneled into scholarships for member institutions, bolstered by sponsorships from partners like Wells Fargo and Coca-Cola. The CIAA also secures grants from local tourism agencies to fund scholarships directly. While the conference has not secured a major national media deal, it continues to benefit from local and regional media interest surrounding its cultural events.

. . .

SIAC: Long-Term Strategy Over High Payouts

While exact revenue figures are less public, the SIAC has built a steady financial model centered on long-term partnerships. A media deal with HBCU Go runs through 2032, providing exposure for football, basketball, and Olympic sports. Sponsors like UBS and Academy Sports fund financial wellness and scholarship programs. Revenue is reinvested into the student-athlete experience more than direct payouts.

HBCUAC: The NAIA's New Financial Model

The HBCUAC, operating within the NAIA, benefits from the Return on Athletics (ROA) model. This approach treats athletics as a potential net revenue generator for institutions. The HBCUAC made headlines for signing the largest media rights deal in NAIA history with Urban Edge Network, alongside a title sponsorship with Hope Credit Union.

Comparison Snapshot: Revenue Distribution Models (2024)

Conference	Approx. Annual Revenue	Distribution Focus	Notable Traits
SWAC	$20M+	Shared + event-specific	Most funded FCS conference
MEAC	$9–13M	Year-end + academic	Academic-based incentives
CIAA	$5–6M	Scholarships + grants	Tournament-driven revenue
SIAC	Not disclosed	Student support + wellness	Long-term strategy focus
HBCUAC	Not disclosed	Institutional ROI	Largest NAIA media deal

These differences reflect not just financial realities but also strategic priorities. Some conferences focus on branding and events, while others focus on education and sustainability. But in every case, the way money flows affects what schools can build, how they can compete, and what they can offer student-athletes.

THE NIL ERA: OPPORTUNITY OR OVERLOAD?

"You don't always have to go D1 to be a good athlete... NIL isn't just for one group. Coming to a D2 school and improving mentally and physically really helped me see that." — *Zoe Ledet, West Virginia State track athlete & content creator*

Historically, HBCU conferences only had to worry about fundraising, visibility, and scheduling. Now, they face something entirely new: paying the athletes.

The introduction of Name, Image, and Likeness (NIL) opportunities and the impending financial obligations from the House v. NCAA settlement have created both a breakthrough and a burden. The House v. NCAA settlement is a landmark legal agreement allowing Division I athletes to receive direct compensation from their schools, shifting college athletics toward a revenue-sharing model similar to professional sports. The ruling comes after years of legal battles over athlete compensation. It is expected to fundamentally reshape how college programs, especially those with limited budgets, fund and manage their athletic departments. On one hand, athletes can now earn money based on their marketability. On the other hand, many HBCUs are scrambling to figure out how to compete in this new financial ecosystem.

The SWAC and MEAC, as Division I conferences, are expected to participate in the NCAA's proposed revenue-sharing structure. This means they may soon be required to allocate hundreds of thousands of dollars per year to compensate athletes directly—money that, in many cases, isn't in the budget. Schools like Morgan State and UMES have already opted into the settlement, signaling their commitment to evolving with the times and acknowledging the financial strain that comes with it.

For Division II and NAIA conferences like the CIAA, SIAC, and HBCUAC, the path forward is murkier. They're not currently required to participate in revenue sharing at the same level, but the pressure to provide competitive NIL opportunities is rising. Student-athletes want access to the same deals, endorsements, and exposure as their counterparts at larger institutions—and many HBCU programs are working overtime to make that happen.

This moment presents both a challenge and an invitation. The challenge is obvious: compete for talent without the deep pockets of Power Five schools. But the invitation is powerful, too. HBCUs can lean into their uniqueness—strong communities, loyal alumni, rich legacies—and build grassroots NIL programs and sponsorship pipelines that reflect their cultural strength.

Whether the NIL era becomes a lifeline or a liability for HBCU sports will depend on how conferences and institutions adapt, collaborate, and communicate their value, not just to sponsors but to the athletes themselves.

West Virginia State sprinter Zoe Ledet built a social media audience of over 1.7 million and secured partnerships with national brands like Target, all while competing at a Division II HBCU. Her story challenges the myth that NIL is only for Division I athletes and shows how dedication, creativity, and community support can open doors for student-athletes at every level.

WHY THESE CONFERENCES MATTER

HBCU athletic conferences do more than set schedules and crown champions. They preserve history. They sustain traditions.

They build and protect spaces where culture, pride, and community can thrive.

They also reveal ongoing challenges. Funding disparities, limited media exposure, and resource gaps compared to predominantly white institutions remain real barriers. Yet, year after year, these conferences continue to generate national impact, not because of external validation but because the communities behind them refuse to let the culture fade.

These conferences aren't just athletic organizations. They are cultural institutions. They represent something bigger than sports: survival, resilience, innovation, and purpose.

Understanding them is understanding the heart of HBCU athletics.

FOUR
HBCU ATHLETES WHO CHANGED HISTORY

You can't tell the story of American sports without telling the story of HBCU athletes.

They forced the spotlight to follow breaking records, breaking barriers, and making sure the rules couldn't stay the same. They redefined how the games were played, who got to play them, and what excellence looked like once the doors finally opened.

Some of these athletes became household names, while others never got the national spotlight they deserved. But all of them carried something bigger than just stats; they held the pride of institutions that refused to be shut out.

Their success wasn't just personal. It was political. It was cultural. It was proof that greatness didn't require mainstream validation, because it had already been built at places most of the country tried to ignore.

TRAILBLAZERS: BUILDING THE ROAD (BEFORE 1970)

Before integration reshaped college and professional sports, HBCU athletes had to find excellence within the walls of their own institutions. Even without mainstream resources, they produced champions, Olympians, and barrier breakers who reached the highest levels of competition.

Audrey Patterson, a standout sprinter from Tennessee State University, made history at the 1948 London Olympics by becoming the first African American woman to win an Olympic medal, earning bronze in the 200 meters. Though often overshadowed by the headlines that followed, Patterson's performance marked a defining moment in Olympic history. It helped launch the Tigerbelle legacy and opened the door for future generations of HBCU women in track and field.

Just days later, Alice Coachman of Tuskegee Institute (now Tuskegee University) took her place in history by becoming the first Black woman from any country to win Olympic gold. Her triumph in the high jump shattered both racial and gender barriers at a time when Black female athletes were almost invisible on the world stage. Coachman's victory captured international attention, and she soon became the first African American woman to sign an endorsement deal with an international company, appearing in Coca-Cola advertisements alongside celebrated white athletes.

Together, Patterson and Coachman didn't just break records; they changed the face of global athletics and redefined what was possible for Black women on the world's biggest stage.

Tank Younger, a fullback from Grambling State, made history in 1949 by becoming the first player from an HBCU to play in the National Football League. Although he wasn't drafted, Younger signed as a free agent with the Los Angeles Rams. Not only did he excel on the field, earning Pro Bowl honors, but he later broke another barrier by becoming the NFL's first African American front office executive.

Bob "Stonewall" Jackson, a standout from North Carolina A&T, followed soon after. In 1950, he became the first player ever drafted from an HBCU when the New York Giants selected him in the 16th round of the NFL Draft. Jackson's selection sent a message the league could no longer ignore: elite football talent was thriving at Black colleges.

Althea Gibson, who attended Florida A&M University, shattered racial barriers in professional tennis. In 1956, she became the first African American to win a Grand Slam title when she captured the French Open. The following year, she won both Wimbledon and the U.S. Nationals (now the U.S. Open), repeating the feat in 1958. Gibson's dominance on the international stage forced segregated tennis into a reckoning and paved the way for generations of Black athletes in traditionally white sports.

Willie Lanier, who starred at Morgan State in the mid-1960s, broke new ground as the first Black middle linebacker to dominate in the NFL—a position often referred to as the "quarterback of the defense." In an era when racial stereotypes questioned Black players' intelligence and leadership capabilities, Lanier's brilliance on the field for the Kansas City Chiefs shattered those narratives, eventually earning him a place in the Pro Football Hall of Fame.

At a time when playing professional sports while Black still came with heavy costs, these men and women didn't just survive. They led.

They changed history.

And by the 1970s, the ripple effects of their contributions began to reshape how the entire sports world measured greatness.

LEGENDS OF THE GAME: DEFINING GREATNESS (1970S–1990S)

By the 1970s and beyond, HBCU athletes were not just entering the national conversation but dominating it.

Walter Payton, a Jackson State University legend, redefined what it meant to be a running back in the NFL. Nicknamed "Sweetness," Payton combined power, grace, and a relentless work ethic. He retired as the league's all-time leading rusher at the time, setting a standard that still shapes the game today.

Andre Dawson, a product of Florida A&M University, took Major League Baseball by storm. Nicknamed "The Hawk," Dawson was an eight-time All-Star, a National League MVP, and a Hall of Famer. His powerful bat and elite defense in center field made him one of the most respected players of his generation.

Jerry Rice didn't just break receiving records out of Mississippi Valley State—he obliterated them. His career totals for receptions, receiving yards, and touchdowns may never be matched. Rice carried the pride of MVSU into every end zone he reached.

Doug Williams, the quarterback from Grambling State, shattered one of the last significant racial barriers in professional football. In 1988, he became the first Black quarterback to start and win a Super Bowl, throwing for a record four touchdowns in one quarter for Washington. His MVP performance remains one of the greatest in Super Bowl history.

Earl "The Pearl" Monroe, who starred at Winston-Salem State University, dazzled basketball fans with his signature flair and creativity. After leading WSSU to a national championship in 1967, he became an NBA legend with the Baltimore Bullets and New York Knicks, earning a spot in the Hall of Fame and helping redefine the guard position.

Chandra Cheeseborough, a sprinter from Tennessee State

University, extended the Tigerbelle legacy into the 1980s. At the 1984 Los Angeles Olympics, she captured two gold medals and one silver while setting a world record in the 4x400m relay. Her accomplishments reaffirmed Tennessee State's status as a cradle of Olympic excellence. Later, she continued the tradition as head coach of TSU's track and field program.

Patricia Hoskins, a scoring phenom from Mississippi Valley State University, dominated women's college basketball in the late 1980s like few players ever have. By the end of her collegiate career, she had racked up 3,122 points and over 1,000 rebounds, setting the NCAA's all-time scoring record. Her career average of 28.4 points per game remains the highest in Division I history—men's or women's. In an era with little media attention for HBCU women's basketball, Hoskins' performances were nothing short of historic. She didn't just lead the nation in scoring, she redefined what dominance looked like from an HBCU program.

Stat Spotlight: Patricia Hoskins (Mississippi Valley State)

- 3,122 career points
- 28.4 PPG – Highest average in NCAA Division I history (men or women)
- 1,000+ rebounds

These athletes didn't just succeed individually. They forced the world to reckon with the talent HBCUs had been producing all along.

MODERN STANDARD-BEARERS: CARRYING THE LEGACY (1990S–PRESENT)

Today, even as the recruiting landscape has shifted, HBCUs continue to produce athletes who leave their mark on the national stage.

Out of Savannah State, Shannon Sharpe dominated as one of the NFL's greatest tight ends. His size, speed, and charisma helped redefine the position, earning him three Super Bowl rings and a place in the Pro Football Hall of Fame.

Tarik Cohen, a dynamic running back from North Carolina A&T, burst onto the NFL scene with the Chicago Bears. His explosive play earned him Pro Bowl honors and showcased the kind of athleticism still thriving at HBCUs.

Terron Armstead, an offensive tackle from the University of Arkansas at Pine Bluff, carved out a reputation as one of the premier linemen in the NFL. A four-time Pro Bowler, Armstead's blend of size, speed, and technique made him a cornerstone for the New Orleans Saints and later the Miami Dolphins.

Rickie Weeks, a slugger from Southern University, dominated college baseball in the early 2000s in a way few players ever have. In 2003, Weeks won the Golden Spikes Award (given to the top amateur baseball player in the country) after leading the NCAA in batting average, home runs, and slugging percentage. He finished his college career with a .465 average, the highest in NCAA history for a three-year player. That same year, the Milwaukee Brewers selected him with the No. 2 overall pick in the MLB Draft, making him the highest-drafted HBCU baseball player ever. Weeks went on to enjoy a decade-long MLB career and brought unprecedented national attention to Black college baseball.

Stat Spotlight: Rickie Weeks (Southern)

- .465 career batting average
- Golden Spikes Award winner (2003)
- No. 2 overall pick in MLB Draft – highest ever for HBCU athlete

Shakyla Hill, the dynamic point guard from Grambling State University, made NCAA history by recording two quadruple-doubles, an almost unheard-of feat at any level of college basketball. But she didn't stop there. After going pro overseas, Hill recorded a third quadruple-double, becoming the only player—male or female—to ever accomplish the feat three times in competitive play. Her highlights went viral, sparking national media attention and proving that HBCU women's basketball wasn't just competitive. It was historic.

Morgan Price, a trailblazing gymnast at Fisk University, made headlines when she turned down Power Five offers to join Fisk's brand-new gymnastics program in 2023. Her bold decision brought instant visibility to the first HBCU women's gymnastics team in history. It sparked a movement around equity, representation, and Black excellence in spaces HBCUs had never been before. Price was also named HBCU Sports' Female Student Athlete of the Year in 2024.

Makur Maker, a five-star basketball recruit, made history in 2020 by choosing to attend Howard University over offers from traditional basketball powerhouses. His decision to commit to an HBCU as a top-tier talent challenged the norms of elite recruiting and sparked a national conversation about the power and potential of Black college programs. Though injuries limited his time on the court, the impact of his choice was seismic, putting Howard basketball and HBCUs at large into the national spotlight in a way that few single decisions ever have.

These modern HBCU athletes aren't just carrying the legacy, but expanding it, proving that HBCU greatness didn't stop with integration. It evolves with every new generation.

OLYMPIC EXCELLENCE: CONQUERING THE WORLD STAGE

The impact of HBCUs isn't just confined to American sports leagues. On the world's biggest athletic stages, HBCU athletes have consistently shown that excellence knows no barriers, as first demonstrated by Olympic pioneers Audrey Patterson and Alice Coachman, two trailblazers already introduced in this chapter who set the stage for everything that followed.

The Tigerbelle Dynasty: Tennessee State's Olympic Legacy

Tennessee State University's track program, known as the Tigerbelles, produced some of the most dominant athletes in Olympic history.

Wilma Rudolph overcame childhood polio to win three gold medals at the 1960 Rome Olympics, becoming an international symbol of perseverance and Black excellence.

Wyomia Tyus became the first athlete—male or female—to defend Olympic gold in the 100 meters, winning titles in 1964 and 1968. She also used her platform to express solidarity with the civil rights movement.

Madeline Manning added to the dynasty with her 800-meter gold in 1968 and a silver medal in the 4x400 relay in 1972. For over 50 years, she remained the only American woman to win Olympic gold in the 800 meters.

Edith McGuire captured gold in the 200 meters and silver medals in both the 100 meters and 4x100 relay at the 1964 Olympics, further solidifying TSU's legacy.

Earlene Brown, also representing Tennessee State, competed

in three Olympics and won bronze in the shot put in 1960, demonstrating that Tigerbelle excellence wasn't limited to the sprints.

INDIVIDUAL GREATS WHO REDEFINED EXCELLENCE

Bob Hayes, the Florida A&M University standout, earned the nickname "The World's Fastest Human" after winning gold medals in the 100-meter and 4x100-meter relay at the 1964 Tokyo Olympics. He later became the only athlete in history to win both an Olympic gold medal and a Super Bowl ring.

Jim Hines of Texas Southern University made Olympic history at the 1968 Mexico City Games when he became the first human to officially run the 100 meters in under 10 seconds. Running the race in 9.95 seconds, he didn't just win a gold medal; he set a world record that no one would touch for 15 years, the longest anyone has held the 100m record in the electronic timing era.

Edwin Moses, a Morehouse College alum, took HBCU Olympic excellence into new territory. Specializing in the 400-meter hurdles, Moses won gold at the 1976 Montreal Olympics and again at the 1984 Los Angeles Olympics. His career included setting world records and winning 107 consecutive finals, marking him as one of the most dominant athletes track and field has ever seen.

Stat Spotlight: Edwin Moses (Morehouse)

- 107 consecutive wins
- 2 Olympic gold medals
- World record holder in the 400m hurdles

Ralph Boston, another Tennessee State legend, succeeded Jesse Owens as the world's top long jumper. He won gold in Rome (1960), silver in Tokyo (1964), and bronze in Mexico City (1968), making him one of the most decorated U.S. Olympians in track and field history.

Lee Calhoun, from North Carolina Central University, made Olympic history by winning back-to-back gold medals in the 110-meter hurdles in 1956 and 1960. He later coached at Grambling State, continuing his influence on HBCU athletics long after his own competition days were over.

Mildred McDaniel, representing Tuskegee Institute, claimed Olympic gold in the high jump at the 1956 Melbourne Games. Her winning leap set a world record, making her the first American woman to do so in the event.

In addition to representing their schools and country, these athletes carried the hopes of generations who had been excluded from opportunity and recognition.

These athletes weren't just competing for medals or glory. They represented generations of Black excellence, built on discipline, sacrifice, and the unshakable belief that greatness wasn't confined by resources or recognition.

Long before the world was ready, they showed up. And by the time the spotlight arrived, the stage was already theirs.

FIVE
COACHES WHO BUILT HBCU GREATNESS

E very legendary HBCU program was built by a coach who turned the playbook into a platform for pride, for discipline, for change. These coaches were mentors, protectors, and life-shapers. They developed athletes who came in with raw talent and left with vision, confidence, and purpose. They turned locker rooms into classrooms, practices into life lessons, and rosters into families. In communities where resources were limited and recognition was scarce, HBCU coaches became father figures, educators, and cultural anchors—all while building programs that could stand toe-to-toe with anyone in the country.

FOOTBALL ARCHITECTS: BUILDING POWERHOUSES FROM THE GROUND UP

Eddie Robinson, the legendary head football coach at Grambling State University, stands as a towering figure in American sports history. He took over the program in 1941 and built it into a football powerhouse despite segregation, underfunding, and limited exposure. Over 57 seasons, Robinson won 408 games—more than any coach in college football history at the time of his retirement. He sent over 200 players to the pros, including Hall of Famers like Buck Buchanan, Willie Davis, Willie Brown, and Charlie Joyner. His teams were beyond dominant. They were disciplined, polished, and prepared for life beyond the game. Robinson proved that excellence didn't need validation, just opportunity.

Jake Gaither at Florida A&M University was another architect of greatness. From 1945 to 1969, Gaither led the Rattlers to six Black college national championships and produced dozens of future NFL stars. Known for his "blood, sweat, and tears" coaching style, he demanded players be "agile, mobile, and hostile." Gaither's influence extended beyond the field, shaping athletic policy and pushing for racial progress during the early years of integration.

William "Billy" Nicks built one of the most dominant dynasties in HBCU football history at Prairie View A&M University. Arriving in 1945, Nicks led the Panthers to seven SWAC championships and six Black college national titles, finishing his tenure at Prairie View with a record of 128-39-8 and a career winning percentage of .787. His programs produced Pro Football Hall of Famer Kenny Houston and Super Bowl champion wide receiver Otis Taylor, two of the most recognizable names to come out of the SWAC in that era. In 1999, he was inducted into the College Football Hall of Fame, and Prairie View A&M named its athletic complex in his honor. His na

While Gaither laid the foundation, it was Rudy Hubbard who delivered FAMU's most historic postseason triumph. As head coach from 1974 to 1985, Hubbard led the Rattlers to the 1978 NCAA Division I-AA national championship. So far, it's the first and only time an HBCU has won a national title at that level. His run through the playoffs didn't just earn respect, it shattered any notion that HBCU programs couldn't compete with the best in the country.

Billy Joe was one of the most successful coaches in HBCU football history, with more than 240 career wins split between Central State University and Florida A&M. At Central State, he won multiple NAIA national championships. At FAMU, he revived the program in the 1990s and led the Rattlers to the NCAA I-AA playoffs seven times. Known for his high-powered offenses and player development, Joe helped transition FAMU from the MEAC to national relevance during a pivotal era.

Affectionately known as "Big John," John Merritt kept the Tennessee State Tigers in the national spotlight from the 1960s through the early '80s. His teams routinely beat PWI opponents and developed NFL greats like Ed "Too Tall" Jones and Joe Gilliam. Merritt's mix of charisma, discipline, and tough love built men as much as it built wins, and his legacy is still felt in the halls of TSU and beyond.

COURT KINGS AND QUEENS: ELEVATING BASKETBALL EXCELLENCE

Clarence "Big House" Gaines left an indelible mark at Winston-Salem State University, coaching for an astonishing 47 seasons. Gaines led the Rams to over 800 career victories and a 1967 NCAA Division II National Championship—the first national championship for any HBCU in NCAA history. Among the players he coached was future NBA Hall of Famer Earl "The Pearl" Monroe, who credited Gaines with transforming him from a raw talent into a polished professional. Gaines wasn't just a winner; he was a builder of opportunities, a fierce advocate for HBCUs, and a mentor who understood that coaching was about shaping lives, not just jump shots.

Cy Alexander quietly built a basketball dynasty at South Carolina State in the 1990s, winning five MEAC titles and reaching the NCAA Tournament five times. He later coached at Tennessee State and North Carolina A&T, elevating every program he touched. Alexander's teams were disciplined, defensive-minded, and resilient, reflecting the identity of the communities they represented.

Davey Whitney, known as "The Wiz," put Alcorn State on the national map in the 1970s and '80s. He led the Braves to multiple NCAA Tournament appearances and made history in 1980 when his squad became the first HBCU to win a game in the NCAA Men's Division I Basketball Tournament. Whitney was known for demanding toughness and accountability, both on and off the court.

Vivian Stringer made her mark at Cheyney State College, leading the women's basketball team to the NCAA Division I Final Four in 1982—the first and only time an HBCU, male or female, has achieved that milestone. Stringer's early coaching career was a masterclass in doing more with less. With few resources and even less recognition, she built a powerhouse that commanded national attention. Her journey eventually took her to Iowa and Rutgers, where she became one of the winningest coaches in NCAA history. But it was at Cheyney, among students who often needed more than a coach, that Stringer first proved that belief could move mountains.

Patricia Cage-Bibbs built a basketball dynasty across multiple HBCU institutions, including Grambling State, Hampton, and North Carolina A&T. With over 500 career victories, Cage-Bibbs became one of the most successful coaches in HBCU history, leading her teams to numerous conference championships and NCAA Tournament appearances. Like Stringer, Cage-Bibbs proved that HBCU women's basketball programs could compete at elite levels despite resource disparities, setting standards of excellence that transformed the programs she touched and elevated the profile of women's basketball throughout HBCU athletics.

Lonnie Bartley turned Fort Valley State University into a women's basketball powerhouse, winning over 600 games during his 32-year coaching career. Under his leadership, the Lady Wildcats captured multiple SIAC titles and became a perennial postseason contender in NCAA Division II. Bartley built his program on discipline, defense, and consistency, often winning with fewer scholarships and less support than his opponents. More than just a coach, he was a mentor and motivator whose influence extended beyond the court, shaping generations of student-athletes and proving that excellence in HBCU women's basketball was not the exception, but the standard.

TRACK TITANS: TURNING CAMPUSES INTO OLYMPIC TRAINING GROUNDS

Ed Temple built one of the most dominant track programs the world has ever seen at Tennessee State University. As head coach of the TSU Tigerbelles, Temple coached athletes like Wilma Rudolph, Wyomia Tyus, and Edith McGuire—women who went on to win Olympic gold and smash world records. Under Temple's leadership, Tennessee State produced 40 Olympic athletes who earned a combined 23 medals. Temple's program thrived despite systemic racism and limited facilities, often training on subpar tracks and second-hand equipment. Yet his athletes consistently outran the world, proving that greatness could flourish anywhere discipline, vision, and belief existed.

LeRoy T. Walker transformed North Carolina Central University into an international track and field force. A scholar, coach, and eventual Olympic administrator, Walker coached over 100 All-Americans and Olympic athletes from multiple nations. He broke barriers as the first Black president of the U.S. Olympic Committee and used his platform to elevate HBCU athletics on the global stage. At NCCU, he blended academic excellence with elite performance, proving that HBCUs could produce both scholars and champions.

George Williams carried the HBCU coaching legacy into the

modern era. At Saint Augustine's University, Williams built a track and field dynasty that dominated Division II athletics. Over his remarkable career, he led Saint Augustine's to 35 NCAA team championships and coached over 400 All-Americans. His athletes won national titles, qualified for the Olympics, and competed globally. In 2004, Williams was named head coach of the U.S. Olympic Track and Field team, a rare honor for any coach, and a profound statement about the excellence coming out of an HBCU. Williams proved that world-class coaching wasn't confined to Division I schools or massive budgets, but that it, too, could thrive at Saint Augustine's.

Victor Thomas continues the legacy of Black coaching excellence at Lincoln University of Missouri, where he has built the Blue Tigers into a Division II track and field powerhouse. A native of Jamaica, Thomas took over the women's program in the mid-1990s and has since led Lincoln to 14 NCAA Division II national championships, including five straight outdoor titles from 2003 to 2007. Known for recruiting internationally and developing overlooked talent, he has created a culture defined by discipline, pride, and performance. His athletes consistently dominate in sprints and relays, challenging programs with far greater resources. At a small HBCU in the Midwest, Thomas is not just winning, he's redefining what success looks like.

DIAMOND DOMINATORS: BUILDING AN HBCU BASEBALL LEGACY

Ralph Waldo Emerson "Prez" Jones was more than just a coach —he was a pioneer. Before becoming president of Louisiana Negro Normal and Industrial Institute (now Grambling State University), Jones laid the foundation for the school's baseball tradition. A strict disciplinarian who valued academics as much as athletics, Jones emphasized character, intellect, and resilience. He helped elevate HBCU baseball during a time when recognition was scarce, setting a standard that coaches after him would continue to build upon.

Roger Cador built Southern University into a Black college baseball powerhouse. Taking over in 1985, Cador led Southern to 14 SWAC titles and 11 NCAA tournament appearances over his 33-year career. His teams routinely beat larger, better-funded programs, sending players to the major leagues and earning national respect. Cador wasn't just building rosters; he was building a movement that demanded recognition for Black college baseball programs long ignored by the mainstream. His success brought cameras, scouts, and fans to the South in a way few had imagined possible for HBCU baseball.

Robert Braddy made history at Jackson State University, serving as head coach from 1973 to 2000. During his legendary tenure, Braddy won 12 SWAC championships and led the Tigers to three NCAA regional appearances. Known for his fierce competitive spirit and ability to develop major league talent, Braddy also became the school's athletic director, helping elevate the university's entire athletic profile. Today, Jackson State's baseball stadium bears his name: Braddy Field.

Wilbert Ellis served as head baseball coach at Grambling State from 1978 to 2003. Throughout his career, Ellis won nearly 750 games and led the Tigers to multiple SWAC championships and NCAA appearances. A teacher at heart, Ellis was known as much for his mentorship and life lessons as his wins. He helped build Grambling's baseball legacy into a national brand and continued serving as an HBCU athletics ambassador long after retirement.

Willie E "Rat" McGowan spent 40 seasons leading the baseball program at Alcorn State University, coaching from 1972 until 2009. Known for his colorful personality and tireless dedication, McGowan amassed over 700 career wins and became one of the longest-tenured coaches in NCAA history. He helped shape generations of Braves players, often with minimal resources, and was widely respected throughout Black college baseball for his loyalty to the game, his athletes, and the HBCU mission.

MODERN STANDARD-BEARERS: CARRYING THE LEGACY

HBCU coaching greatness didn't end with the legends; it evolved. Today's coaches are leading programs through one of the most volatile eras in college athletics history.

They're asked to win on the field, in the classroom, and in the community, while managing the ripple effects of NIL deals, APR restrictions, conference realignment, and the nonstop churn of the transfer portal. It's a job that requires far more than strategy and play-calling. It demands vision, patience, and adaptability.

And yet, these coaches are still delivering.

From Robert Jones at Norfolk State to Donte' Jackson at Alabama A&M, from T.C. Taylor at Jackson State to Trei Oliver at North Carolina Central, from Victor Thomas at Lincoln University (MO) to Dawn Thornton at Alabama A&M, these leaders continue to build winners, develop talent, and mentor young people with purpose. They're not just surviving these modern shifts—they're mastering them.

They carry the baton handed off by legends, proving, every season, that HBCU coaching excellence remains a force.

CLOSING REFLECTIONS: THE LEGACY OF HBCU COACHES

These iconic HBCU coaches redefined what winning meant, turning every locker room into a lab for leadership and every season into a statement of purpose.

Their legacies endure not just in trophies or banners, but in the lives they changed and the communities they empowered.

They proved that leadership doesn't require the biggest stadiums, the fanciest arenas, or the flashiest facilities. It requires vision, resilience, and an unbreakable belief in what's possible.

They transformed coaching into a calling and left a blueprint that still shapes the soul of Black college athletics.

SIX

BLUEPRINT BUILDERS: HBCU PRESIDENTS, COMMISSIONERS & ADS

HBCU athletics didn't thrive just because great players took the field. They thrived because visionary leaders worked behind the scenes, building departments, raising funds, navigating politics, and creating opportunities when no one else would.

While coaches and athletes are often the face of HBCU sports, the administrators and institutional leaders have been the architects. From conference commissioners to university presidents to athletic directors, their decisions have shaped the trajectory of Black college athletics for generations.

Their job hasn't just been about scheduling games or managing budgets; it's been about survival. For decades, HBCU athletic administrators operated with fewer resources, outdated facilities, and little national attention. They worked in systems where television deals, postseason access, and corporate sponsorships were rarely designed with Black colleges in mind. In many cases, they were forced to become fundraisers, marketers, compliance officers, and advocates all at once. And yet, through it all, they found ways to sustain programs, launch new initiatives, and champion student-athletes in a landscape that too often treated HBCUs as an afterthought.

Sometimes their work wasn't just about keeping the lights on. It was about imagining new ways forward.

Take the Celebration Bowl, for example. In 2014, commissioners, athletic directors, and university presidents from the SWAC and MEAC quietly brokered a game-changing agreement. With shrinking TV revenues and limited FCS playoff visibility, HBCU leaders collaborated with ESPN to create a nationally televised postseason bowl game, once again reviving a tradition of HBCUs creating their own stage when none existed."

Morgan State Athletic Director Floyd Kerr confirmed the details in a radio interview, noting that both conferences had voted to move forward with what would become the Celebration Bowl. The goal, he said, was not just to play football but to generate revenue, elevate programs, and control the narrative.

"We have to figure out ways to better fund our programs without taxing the students or the general funds of our institutions, which are already under tremendous fire to increase enrollments, grow revenue [and] graduate students," Kerr explained. "Do you play for a national championship that brings no money and minimal visibility? Or do you create a platform of your own? One that generates revenue and spotlights your school?"

In its debut year, the Celebration Bowl drew over 2.5 million viewers on ABC and generated a reported $1 million in direct payouts to each conference. But beyond the money, it gave HBCUs a nationally televised finale during bowl season. Something few thought possible.

The Celebration Bowl didn't just happen. It was planned, pitched, and protected by HBCU leaders who understood that the future wouldn't wait. Once again, the culture was rewarded, not by asking to be included but by creating something no one else had the vision to build.

COMMISSIONERS WHO CHANGED THE GAME

Long before HBCUs started landing national TV deals or head-lining ESPN Bowl games, there were commissioners doing the quiet work behind the scenes—ensuring Black colleges had influence in rooms where decisions were being made. These were the ones pushing for equity, financial growth, and cultural legitimacy in spaces never built with them in mind.

James Frank, the first African American president of the NCAA and former SWAC commissioner, elevated the profile of HBCU athletics from both within and outside the system. At the NCAA, he championed expanded postseason access. In the SWAC, he laid the groundwork for financial stability through sponsor partnerships.

Ken Free, the MEAC's first full-time commissioner, lobbied for increased TV access and postseason opportunities during a time when Black programs were boxed out. His work helped usher MEAC teams into national broadcasts long before it was trendy.

Dennis Thomas turned a bold vision into action. As MEAC commissioner, he spearheaded the creation of the Celebration Bowl and secured corporate partnerships that made it sustainable. Thomas didn't just get HBCUs in the conversation; he gave them their own spotlight.

Charles McClelland has transformed the SWAC into a 21st-century brand. With record-breaking deals from ESPN, Pepsi, and General Motors, he's not just managing a conference; he's running a cultural enterprise that monetizes history and tradition.

Sonja Stills, the first woman to lead the MEAC, is steering the league through the modern chaos of realignment. Under her leadership, Olympic sports gained new digital platforms, expanding the reach of athletes who often compete in the shadows.

Jacqie McWilliams-Parker, the first woman to lead the CIAA and the first Black woman to serve as commissioner across all NCAA divisions, has made the conference a model for event-driven economics. Her work with Visit Baltimore and partners like Coca-Cola turned a basketball tournament into a city-wide financial engine. Her impact stretches far beyond the scoreboard.

Anthony Holloman is leading a resurgence in the SIAC by blending community investment with modern branding. He's proving that HBCU success can scale without selling out its identity.

And Kiki Baker Barnes is building new blueprints for smaller HBCU programs. Her leadership of the HBCUAC has revitalized NAIA-level schools by modernizing operations, attracting new media attention, and securing strategic partnerships.

While commissioners shaped the landscape, athletic directors transformed individual campuses into powerhouses.

REDEFINING LEADERSHIP: ATHLETIC DIRECTORS PAST & PRESENT

If the commissioners set the stage, the athletic directors ran the playbook. These campus-level leaders made big moves with limited budgets, proving that strategy, innovation, and relationships can take a program further than resources alone. Their work turned local programs into national brands.

Teresa Phillips broke barriers at Tennessee State University as athletic director from 2002 to 2020. In 2003, she became the first woman to coach a Division I men's basketball game. Her leadership transformed TSU athletics through facility improvements, academic success, and enhanced competitive performance, while her NCAA committee service amplified HBCU representation in national athletic governance.

Peggy Davis served as athletic director at Virginia State

University for 20 years and was one of the longest-tenured and most respected women in HBCU athletics. During her time at VSU, she helped guide the Trojans to multiple CIAA championships, strengthened academic support systems for student-athletes, and played a key role in national athletic committees. Davis wasn't loud about her impact, but it was undeniable. She led with strength and consistency, and through her work, she opened doors for the next generation of Black women in college athletics.

At Jackson State, Ashley Robinson turned strategy into spectacle. From landing Deion Sanders to sealing deals with Walmart and American Airlines, he helped JSU break records in revenue, attendance, and cultural clout.

Paul Bryant at Alabama A&M has focused on competitive consistency and infrastructure development. Now at Alabama State, Jason Cable brings years of conference-level insight to campus operations, helping streamline support systems and modernize strategy.

Kery Davis at Howard has built partnerships with elevated visibility and revenue, positioning the Bison as a blueprint for HBCU athletic success in a major media market.

Mikki Allen at Tennessee State University has also redefined what leadership looks like at the HBCU level. In addition to boosting alumni engagement and modernizing TSU's athletic infrastructure, Allen made headlines by launching the first HBCU ice hockey program. This unprecedented move expanded Black college athletics into a completely new space. The initiative, backed by the NHL and NHLPA, signals that HBCUs are not just participating in the traditional model of college sports—they're rewriting it.

Tiffani-Dawn Sykes, athletic director at Virginia State University, represents a new wave of HBCU leadership in the CIAA. With a background in compliance and student-athlete advocacy, Sykes has emphasized academic support, brand development, and strategic partnerships to elevate Virginia State's programs.

Tara Owens at the University of Maryland Eastern Shore has prioritized athlete welfare, alumni engagement, and visibility in non-revenue sports. Under her leadership, UMES has expanded its community footprint and built key partnerships to help the program thrive in a competitive Division I landscape.

Karen Carty, athletic director at the University of the Virgin Islands, is working to elevate the profile of HBCU athletics within the NAIA. With a background in sports information and marketing, Carty has focused on increasing visibility, compliance infrastructure, and student-athlete development across UVI's athletic programs.

A LEGACY OF PRESIDENTIAL VISION

At the top of the pyramid are the university presidents. Leaders who understood that athletics aren't separate from the institutional mission. They're a signal of ambition.

Frederick Humphries, who served as president of Florida A&M University from 1985 to 2001, put FAMU on a bigger stage by moving briefly to Division I-A football, a controversial but courageous attempt to challenge the status quo. His administration also prioritized securing major funding sources for athletics, which included expanding infrastructure and marketing efforts to attract national visibility.

William Harvey, who led Hampton University from 1978 to 2022, showed how realignment can serve institutional growth. He guided Hampton through multiple conference transitions from the CIAA to the MEAC and eventually into the CAA not simply for competition, but to access broader markets, increase brand equity, and leverage athletic success as a fundraising tool. Harvey's vision turned Hampton athletics into a strategic asset.

Walter Washington, president of Alcorn State University

from 1969 to 1992, elevated Alcorn by securing funding for upgraded athletic facilities and standing firmly behind the school's investment in football. His leadership coincided with Alcorn's national rise under Marino Casem, and he helped solidify the university's ability to attract and retain star talent, paving the way for future legends like Steve McNair to thrive.

Makola Abdullah embraced athletics as central to Virginia State's identity. He oversaw major facility upgrades and fostered community support that extended beyond athletics. By hiring Tiffani-Dawn Sykes, he honored a legacy and opened a new chapter rooted in representation, innovation, and elevated standards across the board.

And long before them all, at the very foundation of HBCU athletics, Mary McLeod Bethune laid the groundwork. She didn't just cheer from the sidelines; she shaped the culture of athletics at Bethune-Cookman with her own hands. In 1923, after watching one of the school's early football practices, she is said to have told the players, "You are ferocious. I dub thee the Wildcats." In that moment, the team gained more than a name. They inherited a legacy of pride and excellence that would shape the campus for generations.

Bethune believed that sports could do more than entertain. She thought they could unify a community, develop leadership, and demand respect in a segregated society. Her presence on the sidelines, cane in hand, wasn't symbolic but strategic. She ensured that athletics were seen as integral to Black empowerment and education, embedding both competition and school spirit into the institution's very identity.

CLOSING REFLECTIONS: THEY BUILT THE BLUEPRINT

These leaders weren't chasing headlines. They were chasing sustainability. Their victories were quiet but foundational, laying the groundwork for everything HBCU sports would become. They fought in boardrooms, lobbied for funding, negotiated media deals, and created opportunities where none existed.

They saw athletics not as a distraction from academics, but as a platform to elevate the institution's profile and secure its future.

The builders behind the scenes deserve their place in the story because they made the story possible.

They built the blueprint, and now it's on us to protect it, expand it, and pass it forward.

SEVEN
HBCU FOOTBALL CLASSICS, RIVALRIES, AND COMMUNITY

At HBCUs, football games have never been just football games. They are reunions, parades, fashion shows, business expos, battlefields, and cultural summits rolled into one.

When two HBCUs meet on the field, especially in a classic or traditional rivalry game, they aren't just competing for a win. They're celebrating community, showcasing excellence, and preserving traditions forged during a time when mainstream America ignored Black college sports completely.

In a culture where visibility, pride, and identity were often contested on every front, HBCU classics and rivalries gave Black colleges a stage to shine on their own terms. They still do.

The earliest HBCU classics were born out of necessity. During the era of Jim Crow segregation, Black colleges were excluded from participating in bowl games, major postseason tournaments, and national media coverage. In response, HBCUs created their own showcase events. The kind of games that would crown their own champions, draw massive crowds, and generate revenue for their institutions.

Classics quickly became cultural institutions in their own

right. They weren't simply athletic contests. They were full-day experiences: parades in the morning, tailgates by noon, battles of the bands at halftime, and after-parties that stretched long into the night. For many Black families and communities, attending a classic was as important as attending a graduation or a church homecoming. These games weren't about standings; they were about showing up, showing pride, and showing that Black colleges were producing excellence academically, athletically, and culturally.

THE CLASSICS: CULTURE ON DISPLAY

Several HBCU Classics have become nationally recognized events, drawing tens of thousands of fans annually and generating millions in economic impact for their host cities:

• **The Bayou Classic**: Grambling State vs. Southern University. Played annually in New Orleans since 1974, the Bayou Classic isn't just a football game, it's a cultural phenomenon. National broadcasts, massive tailgates, and the iconic Battle of the Bands make it the pinnacle of HBCU sports pageantry.

• **The Magic City Classic**: Alabama A&M vs. Alabama State. Held in Birmingham, it draws over 60,000 fans and includes scholarship breakfasts, parades, and step shows. It's a complete weekend of celebration.

• **The Florida Classic**: Bethune-Cookman vs. Florida A&M. Played in Orlando, it often attracts over 50,000 fans and highlights the musical and athletic excellence of two storied Florida programs.

• **The Turkey Day Classic**: Alabama State vs. Tuskegee (and other matchups). Dating back to 1924, it's the oldest known HBCU classic and historically provided a postseason-like stage for Black athletes.

• **The State Fair Classic**: Grambling State vs. Prairie View

A&M. Played at the Cotton Bowl in Dallas, it blends football with the excitement of the Texas State Fair.

• **The Circle City Classic**: Launched in 1984 in Indianapolis with rotating teams, this game brought Southern traditions to the Midwest with step shows, band battles, and HBCU pride.

• **The Fountain City Classic**: Albany State vs. Fort Valley State. A Georgia-based matchup that unites alumni and local supporters in a celebration of heritage and tradition.

• **The MEAC/SWAC Challenge**: Established in 2005, this nationally televised game features a representative from each conference. It kicks off the season and showcases elite HBCU talent.

MORE THAN A GAME: WHAT THESE CLASSICS MEAN TO US

For those of us who attended Grambling or Southern, the Bayou Classic isn't just a football game. It's the centerpiece of the entire Thanksgiving holiday weekend. While most families plan their Thanksgiving celebrations and then decide what to do afterward, it's the reverse for us. We plan Thanksgiving around the Bayou Classic. Some folks skip the traditional dinner altogether. Others come into New Orleans early—on Wednesday or even earlier—and opt to have Thanksgiving at a restaurant if they can find one open, just so they're rested and ready for everything that kicks off the next day. That's how serious this weekend is. It goes far beyond the game. It's about the music, the memories, the deep-rooted tradition, and the pride of watching your school take the spotlight in a city that feels like home every year.

Richelle Williams, an Alabama A&M alumna, shared her deep-rooted connection to the Magic City Classic: "My dad graduated from Alabama A&M, my brother did, I have uncles that graduated from A&M, I graduated from Alabama A&M.

I've been attending the Classic probably for the last 50 years. I brought my daughter with me now. She's 14. She's been coming probably the last couple of years also, but I want her to see how the Classic really is as a teenager now."

Xavier Lankford, quarterback for Alabama A&M, echoed that sense of connection: "My grandmother lives not that far from the stadium, maybe a ten-minute walk from the stadium. I've been a part of many classics even before playing for A&M, so I know exactly what this game means. Coming home, seeing family, friends that I haven't seen all year, it means a lot. Just going out and producing the right way, that's what I'm excited to do."

That's the power of these gatherings. They're not just marked on calendars, they're woven into family stories. They're the backdrop for first dates, fraternity strolls, and a baby's first band dance. You don't just go. You come back louder. Sharper. Ready to represent.

Classics like these live on not because of the score, but because of the feeling. It's that charge you feel when you're back with your people. The sound. The environment. The history. And none of it is borrowed either. It's all ours.

FROM RADIO TO REELS: MEDIA THAT MOVES THE CULTURE

Long before the cameras showed up, HBCU Classics were community events spread by word of mouth, flyers, and the Black press. In many towns, the only way to follow the game was to crowd around an AM radio, listen for updates from the local station, or wait for the Monday edition of the *Pittsburgh Courier* or *Chicago Defender*. Local sportswriters and radio hosts carried the weight of community storytelling, capturing not just the score but the feeling in the stands.

That all changed in 1991 when the Bayou Classic made history as the first HBCU football game to be broadcast nationally. NBC's decision to televise the game brought HBCU football—and its cultural spectacle—to millions of homes across the country. It wasn't just a game on TV. It was validation that HBCU traditions had value, entertainment power, and national appeal.

During the late 1990s and early 2000s, BET also played a crucial role in broadcasting HBCU games, band showcases, and highlight packages. These broadcasts helped embed the sounds of marching bands and the visuals of step teams into mainstream media. But as TV rights shifted and attention moved elsewhere, many HBCUs found themselves without national coverage again.

Today, digital platforms have leveled the playing field. Streaming services like ESPN+, HBCU GO, and local university-run YouTube channels have filled the gap. Not only are games more accessible to alumni and fans nationwide, but creators have emerged to document the entire HBCU game day experience, from the halftime show to the tailgate. Independent platforms like *HBCU Sports* (hbcusports.com) and other fan-led YouTube creators have become modern-day storytellers, often providing more consistent and culturally accurate coverage than mainstream outlets.

Even student-athletes and marching band members are becoming media channels in their own right. Through TikTok, Instagram Reels, and personal YouTube vlogs, they're giving audiences a behind-the-scenes look at life within HBCU programs, often generating viewership numbers that rival traditional regional sports broadcasts or cable coverage.

The evolution of media coverage hasn't just improved visibility. It has helped preserve the cultural importance of these events and ensure that HBCU excellence is seen, heard, and felt nationally, often led by Black-owned platforms and creators who understood the value of the culture long before the networks did.

RIVALRIES THAT RUN DEEP

Beyond formal "Classics," some rivalries are stitched into the DNA of HBCU sports culture. Among them:

• **The Soul Bowl** (Jackson State vs. Alcorn State): A family affair steeped in Mississippi's racial, cultural, and football history, this rivalry draws fierce passion across generations.

• **The Aggie-Eagle Classic** (North Carolina A&T vs. North Carolina Central): This heated contest of regional pride and tradition dates back to the 1920s and represents one of the most electric atmospheres in HBCU sports.

• **The Battle of the Real HU** (Howard vs. Hampton): More than a battle of initials, this rivalry is about prestige, legacy, and the constant debate over cultural influence.

• **The BoomBox Classic** (Jackson State vs. Southern University): Named for the Sonic Boom of the South and the Human Jukebox marching bands, this game blends musical pageantry and athletic intensity into a can't-miss experience.

These rivalries aren't just about bragging rights. They are about identity, family ties, alumni pride, and generational storytelling. They pack stadiums even when championships aren't on the line, proving that the stakes are measured not just by records, but by culture and legacy.

WHEN CULTURE PAYS: THE BUSINESS OF THE CLASSICS

HBCU Classics don't just bring alumni together. They bring dollars into Black communities. These games generate real economic activity, from tailgate vendors and food trucks to local hotels and Black-owned businesses.

According to the Greater Birmingham Convention & Visitors Bureau, the Magic City Classic generates more than $25 million in economic impact for the city annually. Similarly, the Bayou Classic has produced as much as $50 million for the city of New Orleans. The Florida Classic contributes an estimated $30 million yearly to the Orlando economy. Combined, these and other classics generate over $100 million annually, making HBCU football not just an event but an economic force.

But the benefits extend beyond stadium walls. Street vendors, event planners, DJs, step show hosts, fashion designers, and pop-up merch booths all find opportunity at these gatherings. It's not just game day. It's Black Business Day.

As major sponsors and outside event management firms begin to take an interest, questions of ownership and cultural control grow louder. There's real concern that the soul of these events could be diluted as corporations seek to profit without reinvesting in the communities that made these gatherings iconic. HBCUs and their alumni networks must remain vigilant, ensuring the culture stays at the center as these events scale.

In a world where HBCUs have always had to build their own systems, these classics have become one of the few consistent spaces where culture, community, and commerce align. The games matter. The traditions matter. But the economic footprint matters just as much.

PROTECTING THE LEGACY

In a world where Black institutions have often been denied traditional platforms, HBCU classics remain a space where tradition, community, and Black excellence are celebrated on our terms. They're about ownership, culture, and building wealth and legacy where it matters most.

That's why these games are more than events on a calendar. They reflect who we are, what we've built, and why the culture will never be sidelined again. Whether we know it or not, every child in the crowd is learning what excellence looks like when it belongs to us. I know from personal experience. I remember seeing it myself as a kid.

EIGHT

THE LEGACY AND DECLINE OF THE HBCU–NFL PIPELINE

BEFORE THE DRAFT NOTICED BLACK COLLEGES

Tank Younger, a fullback from Grambling, signed with the Los Angeles Rams as an undrafted free agent in 1949. He became a four-time Pro Bowler and one of the NFL's first Black front-office executives. His success, and the success of others who followed, forced professional football to reckon with the obvious: HBCUs were producing elite talent at a time when the nation's biggest programs were still wrestling with racial integration.

Younger's path to the league also revealed how crucial belief and negotiation were in opening doors. After being overlooked in the NFL Draft, Rams scout Eddie Kotal traveled to Grambling to sign him. Sitting with Coach Eddie Robinson and school president Dr. Ralph Waldo Emerson Jones, the group discussed Younger's potential contract. Kotal suggested offering $4,000—the lower end of the rookie pay scale—to improve his odds of making the roster. Robinson pushed back firmly: "Give him $6,000 and if he isn't good enough, cut him." That moment mattered. Younger hadn't even dreamed of earning that much to play football.

Long before Black athletes were welcomed into the major college football programs at predominantly white institutions, HBCUs were developing world-class football talent. Yet, for much of the early 20th century, professional scouts, team executives, and national media simply ignored that reality. Black players from HBCUs, no matter how talented, were often overlooked in favor of white players from PWIs. Those who did make it to the NFL usually arrived through sheer perseverance, personal connections, or backdoor opportunities rather than formalized scouting systems.

THE GOLDEN ERA: HBCUS TAKE OVER THE NFL DRAFT

The NFL Draft is often portrayed as the ultimate validation of college football excellence. It's the moment when raw talent, hard work, and national attention intersect. However, for HBCUs, the NFL Draft has always been about more than professional dreams. It has been about access. About proving worth in a system that spent decades pretending not to see it. About survival, pride, and the relentless pursuit of respect.

In 1950, Bob "Stonewall" Jackson of North Carolina A&T became the first player from an HBCU to be selected in the NFL Draft when the New York Giants picked him in the 16th round. Jackson's selection cracked open a door that future HBCU legends would soon walk through and kick wide open.

The 1960s and 1970s marked the golden era of HBCUs in the NFL Draft. Players like Walter Payton (Jackson State), Jerry Rice (Mississippi Valley State), Deacon Jones (South Carolina State), Shannon Sharpe (Savannah State), and Michael Strahan (Texas Southern) didn't just make NFL rosters; they redefined what excellence looked like at their positions. These athletes shattered records, earned Hall of Fame enshrinement, and became global icons. They carried with them not only the pride of their institutions but the pride of generations of Black athletes who had been denied their rightful place for so long.

At its peak, the NFL Draft featured as many as 30–40 HBCU players in a single year. In 1974 alone, 36 players from Black colleges were selected. Teams like the Pittsburgh Steelers, Oakland Raiders, and Los Angeles Rams routinely mined the SWAC and MEAC for game-changing athletes.

HALL OF FAME LEGACY: HBCUS ON FOOTBALL'S BIGGEST STAGE

The NFL Draft opened the door, but it was on the field that HBCU athletes made their case permanent. Many of the legends who came through Black college programs during the Golden Era didn't just make rosters. They made history and earned enshrinement in Canton.

- **Willie Davis** (Grambling State): A five-time NFL champion and anchor of Vince Lombardi's defense in Green Bay. He became one of the first Black football stars in a historically white franchise.
- **Deacon Jones** (South Carolina State / Mississippi Valley State): A dominant pass rusher who coined the term "sack" and revolutionized the defensive end position.
- **Buck Buchanan** (Grambling State): The first Black player ever drafted No. 1 overall, and a force in the trenches for the Kansas City Chiefs.
- **Mel Blount** (Southern University): A lockdown cornerback whose physical play led to rule changes and four Super Bowl wins with the Steelers.
- **Art Shell** (Maryland Eastern Shore): Not only a Hall of Fame lineman but one of the NFL's first Black head coaches.
- **Walter Payton** (Jackson State): Nicknamed "Sweetness,"

he retired as the league's all-time leading rusher and remains one of the most admired players in football history.

• **John Stallworth** (Alabama A&M): Drafted by the Steelers in 1974, he became a go-to deep threat in one of the most dominant dynasties in NFL history.

• **Jerry Rice** (Mississippi Valley State): Widely considered the greatest wide receiver in NFL history. He holds the all-time records for receptions, receiving yards, and touchdowns.

Their presence in the Pro Football Hall of Fame is more than symbolic. It's evidence that HBCUs didn't just produce NFL players; they produced legends.

A generation of Hall of Famers from HBCUs didn't just define their positions. They helped define an era of football. Their rise coincided with a period of transformation across college athletics and professional scouting.

THE SHIFT: INTEGRATION CHANGES EVERYTHING

The very progress that opened doors at PWIs also reshaped the HBCU sports landscape. The passage of the Civil Rights Act of 1964 led to the gradual desegregation of college athletics. As major universities across the South began integrating in the late 1960s and 1970s, the recruitment of Black athletes shifted dramatically. Suddenly, HBCUs were competing for the same elite talent they once had exclusive access to, only now, without their new competitors' budgets, facilities, or media spotlight.

THE FALLOUT: DECLINE, OVERSIGHT, AND LOST VISIBILITY

Over time, the talent pipeline shifted. HBCUs still produced NFL players, but the numbers began to dwindle. In recent decades, that decline has become even more pronounced. In 2021, for the first time in over a decade, not a single HBCU player heard his name called during the NFL Draft. An unthinkable silence for institutions that once served as the league's greatest talent pipeline.

HBCU NFL Draft Picks by Year
- 1974: 36 players
- 1984: 20 players
- 1994: 17 players
- 2004: 8 players
- 2014: 4 players
- 2021: 0 players
- 2022: 4 players
- 2023: 1 player
- 2024: 2 players
- 2025: 1 player

Source: HBCU Sports (2025)

Yet this trend isn't unique to HBCUs. The overall number of players selected from the Football Championship Subdivision (FCS) and Division II levels, including those from PWIs, has dropped as NFL teams concentrate on players from Power Four programs. However, what makes the HBCU gap more glaring is that this talent pipeline once helped build the league.

THE COMEBACK TRAIL: LEGACY BOWL & MODERN HOPES

Recognizing the need to address the imbalance, HBCU advocates and NFL partners have launched strategic initiatives to reclaim this legacy. One of the most significant is the creation of the HBCU Legacy Bowl, an annual postseason all-star game dedicated to showcasing the top draft-eligible players from HBCUs. Founded by the Black College Football Hall of Fame in partnership with the NFL, the Legacy Bowl provides critical exposure, allowing athletes to perform directly in front of pro scouts and executives.

Since its launch in 2022, the Legacy Bowl has featured dozens of prospects, many of whom earned NFL camp invites or landed on practice squads. The game isn't just a showcase, it's a signal that HBCU talent deserves intentional visibility.

Meanwhile, individual athletes continue to break through:

• **Darius Leonard** (South Carolina State): 2018 2nd-round pick, multiple-time All-Pro

• **James Houston IV** (Jackson State): 2022 6th-round pick, breakout rookie season with the Detroit Lions

• **Coby Durant** (South Carolina State): 4th-round pick in 2022, contributing with the Los Angeles Rams

• **Grover Stewart** (Albany State): Undrafted, now a starting defensive tackle for the Indianapolis Colts

These stories prove the talent never left—only the spotlight did. The excellence remained. The hunger never left either.

NFL FRANCHISES THAT EMBRACED HBCU TALENT

Some NFL teams didn't just take chances on HBCU players; they built legacies with them.

• **Pittsburgh Steelers:** Drafted multiple HBCU stars in the 1970s, including Hall of Famer Donnie Shell (South Carolina State) and wide receiver John Stallworth (Alabama A&M). Shell was undrafted and went on to become a four-time Super Bowl champion. Stallworth became a go-to target for Terry Bradshaw and played a key role in the team's dynasty.

• **Los Angeles Rams:** Made history by signing Grambling's Tank Younger in 1949—the first HBCU player to reach the NFL.

Later, they would also draft standout players like Isiah Robertson (Southern University), a six-time Pro Bowler.

• **Oakland Raiders:** Under Al Davis, the Raiders were among the most aggressive in scouting HBCUs. The team signed players like Art Shell (Maryland Eastern Shore), who would become a Hall of Fame offensive tackle and one of the first Black head coaches in the modern NFL.

• **Kansas City Chiefs:** Drafted Buck Buchanan out of Grambling State with the first overall pick in the 1963 AFL Draft. Buchanan was the first Black player ever taken No. 1 overall in any professional football draft. He became a cornerstone of their Super Bowl IV defense and a Hall of Famer.

These teams weren't just scouting differently. They were changing the league, and, in some cases, the front office.

One of the most powerful but lesser-known moments from this era came in 1977, when Los Angeles Rams owner Carroll Rosenbloom offered Eddie Robinson the opportunity to become the first Black head coach in the modern NFL. At the time, Robinson had already built Grambling into a football power-house and was widely respected across the sport. But he turned the offer down. Not because he wasn't qualified, but because he believed his purpose was rooted at Grambling to develop young men and continue lifting an entire institution. Robinson's decision reflected a deeper truth about HBCU athletics: it was never just about getting to the league. It was about building something so powerful, the league had no choice but to take notice.

THE FUTURE OF HBCUS IN PRO FOOTBALL

Carson Vinson, an offensive lineman from Alabama A&M, was selected by the Baltimore Ravens in the 2025 NFL Draft. Like Payton and Younger before him, Vinson isn't just representing a school—he's carrying a legacy. In an interview shortly after being drafted, he reflected on what it meant to carry the HBCU banner to the next level:

"Being from an HBCU, it's so special. Over this entire process, once HBCU guys get past our rivalries and teams, we're all one big family. I've gotten support from every single HBCU team, especially after I got the Senior Bowl invite. After games, guys would tell me, 'Hey, you're gonna do great things.'"

He also emphasized why he stayed at Alabama A&M all four years:

"With the transfer portal and the way things are, a lot of guys feel like they have to transfer up to get where they want to go. But it was really important to me to stay. Those were the best four years of my life. You can go anywhere you want from the institution that you're at."

Still, the road back to NFL Draft prominence for HBCUs won't be paved by publicity alone. Without the same NIL visibility and booster backing as larger schools, HBCUs often fight to keep talent on campus long enough to develop draft potential. It will require continued investment in facilities, strategic media partnerships, improved athletic budgets, and a renewed understanding that greatness has always existed at HBCUs—and still does.

The history, the talent, and the foundation are already in place. What's needed now is exposure, infrastructure, and commitment.

The history of HBCU players and the NFL Draft is not just a footnote in American sports. It's a story of systemic exclusion, relentless perseverance, and transformative excellence. It's the story of Black athletes refusing to be overlooked and of institutions that believed in them long before the spotlight ever found them.

The path from HBCUs to the NFL may look different than it did fifty years ago. Yet recent social justice movements have renewed national attention toward HBCUs, sparking new conversations, new investments, and new opportunities. That increased visibility has the potential to open doors not just for athletes but for entire athletic programs.

However, the mission remains the same: to create opportunity, showcase excellence, and demand respect—not just on draft day but every time a Black athlete steps on the field. Just like Eddie Robinson did in 1949, we're still negotiating for our value and still proving we've always been worth the investment.

NINE

THE RISE OF HBCU POSTSEASON FOOTBALL

For decades, HBCUs were expected to follow rules they didn't write, chase playoff bids they rarely received, and participate in systems that often excluded their priorities, culture, and communities. So they did what they've always done: they built something of their own.

There were breakthrough moments, most notably in 1978, when head coach Rudy Hubbard led Florida A&M University to victory in the inaugural NCAA Division I-AA (now FCS) national championship, defeating UMass 35–28. FAMU remains the only HBCU ever to claim that title, proving that when given access, HBCUs didn't just compete, they won.

But moments like that were the exception. Most postseason formats continued to marginalize HBCUs, offering little exposure, limited financial return, and no alignment with the cultural heartbeat of Black college football. Invitations were scarce. Visibility was minimal. The returns, both economic and reputational, were rarely worth the investment.

This chapter isn't just about bowl games or trophies—it's about independence. It's about saying no to structures that don't serve you and building ones that do. It's about celebrating the game on your own terms, culturally, strategically, and financially.

BEFORE THE SYSTEM LET THEM IN

Before the Pelican Bowl kicked off in New Orleans, HBCUs were already creating postseason games.

There were no playoff brackets. No selection committees. No shot at the big-name bowls. But that didn't mean Black college football programs sat quietly in the corner. They did what they've always done—made their own lane.

National titles weren't handed out by the NCAA. They were claimed in Black newspapers, barbershop debates, and Sunday conversations after church. The *Pittsburgh Courier,* arguably the most respected Black publication in America at the time, started naming Black college national champions as early as the 1920s. Their rankings weren't based on politics or access. They were based on wins, schedules, and pride. And when the Courier named your school No. 1, it mattered.

Other polls followed. Some were official. Some were personal, but the point was always the same: HBCUs didn't need anyone's validation to know who the best was.

And while the postseason wasn't structured like today, there were still games that meant everything.

The Orange Blossom Classic in Miami? That was the Super Bowl for Black college football long before the term existed. FAMU made it a destination, but it was bigger than one school. It was where reputations were built and history was written.

There were others, too. Regional matchups like the Prairie View Bowl, the Steel Bowl, and the Vulcan Bowl drew crowds, and some faded with time. But they all played a role in keeping HBCU football in the spotlight, even if that spotlight was created by the community itself.

And then there was 1948, when Southern University flew out

to California and beat San Francisco State in the Fruit Bowl, a team from an all-Black school taking down a predominantly white one on their turf. That wasn't just a win. That was a statement.

So when the Pelican Bowl came around in the '70s, it wasn't a radical idea. It was just the latest move in a long tradition of HBCUs refusing to wait for anyone's approval. They'd been running their own postseason. They'd been crowning their own champions. They just wanted something that looked a little more official.

But make no mistake; what came before the Pelican Bowl wasn't just history. It was foundation.

THE PELICAN BOWL (1972–1975)

In 1972, HBCUs took their first significant swing at postseason autonomy with the launch of the Pelican Bowl, a proposed show-down between the SWAC and MEAC champions in New Orleans' Tulane Stadium.

The concept carried real symbolic and political weight. It wasn't just a football game—it was a statement of pride and purpose. But the event's execution faced challenges. The NCAA refused to sanction the event, conference tensions ran high, and team participation was inconsistent. Meanwhile, the rise of the Bayou Classic pulled away from the Pelican Bowl's focus and energy. And by 1975, the bowl game had folded.

Still, the Pelican Bowl left behind more than a short history; it introduced a mindset: HBCUs didn't have to wait to be invited to postseason stages. They could build their own.

THE HERITAGE BOWL (1991–1999)

The Heritage Bowl followed that spirit, launching in 1991 under the leadership of MEAC Commissioner Ken Free and SWAC

Commissioner James Frank. Backed by the National Urban League and broadcast nationally on BET and CBS, it was positioned to crown a definitive Black college football national champion.

The idea was sound. The stage was visible. But consistent buy-in proved elusive. MEAC champions often declined invites in favor of FCS playoff bids, leading to anticlimactic matchups and missed opportunities. For MEAC teams, the decision often came down to chasing national validation through the FCS playoffs or honoring tradition and community through the Heritage Bowl—a choice that exposed the tension between visibility and value.

Still, the Heritage Bowl proved something critical: there was demand, an audience, and cultural weight. Even in its inconsistencies, the bowl reaffirmed that HBCU football deserved a postseason that reflected its values and vision.

THE SWAC CHAMPIONSHIP GAME (1999–PRESENT)

When Rudy Washington took over as SWAC Commissioner in 1998, he didn't just inherit a conference, he inherited an opportunity. In 1999, with approval from the SWAC Council of Presidents, Washington helped launch the league's first-ever football championship game. But there was a tradeoff: the SWAC had to give up its automatic bid to the FCS playoffs.

That tradeoff wasn't a sacrifice. It was strategy.

The SWAC could now crown its champion based on the outcome of a postseason matchup, control its postseason schedule, and create an event tailored to its culture. Initially, the winner advanced to the Heritage Bowl. However, when the NCAA banned teams from participating in multiple postseason games starting in 2000, the Heritage Bowl folded, but the SWAC title game remained.

What began in Birmingham's Legion Field later moved to Houston's NRG Stadium and eventually to the campuses of top-seeded teams. The shift to campus sites wasn't originally the plan, but circumstances forced the SWAC's hand. In 2018, the conference had booked Legion Field for the championship game, but a last-minute scheduling conflict emerged when UAB, which shares the venue, needed it for its own game. With limited time to find a neutral site, SWAC Commissioner Charles McClelland and his team moved the game to Alcorn State, the top-seeded representative from the East Division.

The move worked. Attendance improved, expenses dropped, and the fan experience took on a new energy level. That one-year adjustment became the new model going forward, proving that you don't need an NFL stadium to create a championship experience that feels big, connected, and culturally grounded.

What the FCS Playoffs Don't Offer	Details
Financial Incentives	• No payout for participating teams
Hosting Costs	• Home teams must pay $30,000–$40,000 in bidding fees
Revenue Sharing	• NCAA takes 85% of ticket revenue
Media Visibility	• Limited television exposure, especially in early rounds
Fan Engagement	• Sparse attendance in early-round games
Cultural Representation	• No space for halftime shows, marching bands, or other HBCU traditions

The decision to forgo the FCS playoffs also made financial sense. Hosting a playoff game can cost schools between $30,000 and $40,000 in bidding fees, with 85% of ticket revenue going back to the NCAA. That's a tough sell for athletic departments already strapped for cash.

By contrast, the SWAC Championship Game is a self-contained asset. It draws national broadcasts on ESPN, attracts title sponsors, and routinely generates attendance numbers that rival FBS conference title games. It's not just a win for the champion, it's a win for the entire conference.

Since 2015, the SWAC title game has also served as the play-in to the Celebration Bowl, effectively making it the conference's gateway to a national championship.

THE CELEBRATION BOWL (2015–PRESENT)

For years, HBCUs were told to chase legitimacy through cold stadiums, low payouts, and quiet exits. There were no bands. No community. Just elimination. By contrast, the Celebration Bowl offers a national stage, cultural relevance, and a payout that supports long-term sustainability.

The Celebration Bowl, launched by ESPN Events in 2015, is now the premier postseason event in Black college football. Held annually in Atlanta and broadcast nationally on ABC, it matches the champions of the SWAC and MEAC in a bowl-style showdown for a mythical Black College Football National Championship.

But it wasn't simply gifted to HBCUs, it was earned through leadership and negotiation. Heading into the sixth annual Celebration Bowl, his last as MEAC Commissioner, Dennis Thomas reflected on a moment that captured it all.

"He called me over and he said, 'Commissioner, I'm so happy that you didn't give up on your vision,'" Thomas recalled of a conversation with North Carolina A&T head coach Rod Broadway. "'Because see what our kids experienced, see what our alumni experienced, see the institutions, our branding, the promotion, the marketing—the world saw it. If you had given up on your vision, this wouldn't have happened.'"

Thomas added, "That crystallized everything for me."

Each conference reportedly receives a $1 million payout. Schools don't have to bid to host. Instead of competing in front of modest crowds in FCS stadiums, they perform under bright lights during bowl season, in front of national audiences. The experience, on the field, in the stands, and at the surrounding events, feels distinctly HBCU.

Critics argue that opting out of the FCS playoffs removes HBCUs from the larger national championship conversation. But the Celebration Bowl does something the playoffs never have: It centers HBCU football. The bands, the pageantry, the stakes— everything is aligned with Black college football's cultural DNA.

After leading North Carolina A&T to victory in the inaugural Celebration Bowl, head coach Rod Broadway summed it up plainly:

"I thought it was a beautiful thing what (MEAC Commissioner Dennis Thomas) did and (Pete Derzis, Sr. VP of ESPN Events) and all those guys, fighting for this thing and getting people in the MEAC to agree to it, because it's a beautiful experience. To me, and this is just my opinion, I'm not speaking for anyone except me. There's so much more value in this (the Celebration Bowl) than the playoffs for us because we're not financed to win national championships at this time, but we are … good enough to win this championship."

He added, "Any push back they got, that's old news, man. We're proud to be a part of this bowl situation."

There's one caveat: the Celebration Bowl is owned by ESPN. And while the network has elevated HBCU visibility, the event's future ultimately rests in corporate hands. Should the partnership end, the infrastructure and funding would have to be rebuilt. That's the tradeoff—exposure in a space you don't fully control.

Still, for now, it stands as a model of what's possible when HBCUs define their own postseason.

DIVISION II DESERVES A STAGE TOO

Not all HBCUs compete in Division I, but every HBCU deserves a postseason spotlight.

That was the idea behind the Pioneer Bowl, launched in 1997 as a postseason contest between the CIAA and SIAC programs that missed out on the Division II playoffs. It was a culturally relevant, competitive alternative that gave athletes a tangible postseason goal.

But like many bold HBCU initiatives, the Pioneer Bowl struggled with sustainability. Shifting host cities, sponsor issues, and canceled games chipped away at its momentum. It folded quietly in 2014.

Nearly a decade later, the Florida Beach Bowl emerged with new energy. Backed by Amerant Bank and broadcast on HBCU Plus and the Impact Network, it aimed to revive the Pioneer Bowl's purpose with stronger infrastructure. Its inaugural game between Fort Valley State and Johnson C. Smith in 2023 reportedly reached over 720,000 viewers.

The surrounding events, including media day, fan festivals, and luncheons, signaled a broader vision: to build a Celebration Bowl–style experience for Division II HBCUs.

But in 2024, that vision hit a wall. The game was canceled due to funding shortfalls. A reminder that big dreams require long-term investment. Still, the interest is real. The audience exists. The moment is waiting. The opportunity is real. With support, it could become for Division II what the Celebration Bowl is for Division I, a high-stakes, culture-driven showcase for the CIAA and SIAC.

MORE THAN JUST A GAME

Each bowl, championship, or postseason innovation described in this chapter reveals a single truth: HBCUs have always found a way to elevate their programs, whether or not the larger system recognized their value.

At every level, these postseason efforts share a common thread: they're about ownership. They're about refusing to be afterthoughts in someone else's structure. They're about elevating tradition while building new systems rooted in culture, autonomy, and value.

HBCUs may not dominate the FCS playoff headlines. But they've created something far more resonant—a postseason that feels like them, sounds like them, and serves their communities.

That's more than a workaround.

That's power.

And it goes beyond football. What HBCUs have built in postseason play is a blueprint for cultural preservation and institutional self-reliance. It's a reminder that when traditional systems fall short or actively exclude, Black institutions don't just survive. They innovate. They lead. And they create platforms that reflect their own priorities, values, and vision for the future.

TEN

HBCU BANDS: THE SOUNDTRACK OF BLACK COLLEGE FOOTBALL

I f you've ever been to an HBCU football game, you know this truth: the band isn't background noise. It's the heartbeat. From the first blast of the horns during warmups to the last note in the Fifth Quarter, HBCU bands set the tone, command the moment, and leave fans with memories that often outshine the game itself.

For generations, these bands have done more than play music. They've built culture, shaped school identity, and elevated game day into a full-on spectacle. They're why people show up early. They're why people stay late. And in many cases, they're why people come at all.

A CULTURE WITHIN A CULTURE

The tradition of Black college marching bands goes back to the 1890s. Tuskegee started it in 1894 under student leadership, planting the seeds for what would become a defining part of HBCU culture. It didn't take long for other schools to follow. Once leaders like Nathaniel Clark Smith and W.C. Hardy brought military structure and musical flair into the mix, a new kind of performance art was born.

By the 1940s and '50s, schools like Florida A&M and Grambling were rewriting the playbook. High steps. Hip swings. Choreography. Soul. The field was no longer just for football—it became a stage. HBCU bands fused classical training with African-American musical traditions, spirituals, jazz, and R&B. That fusion didn't just resonate in the stadium—it bled into American popular culture.

These bands weren't just entertaining their schools. They were representing the culture on national stages: Tennessee State on TV in the '50s, Grambling at the first Super Bowl, and most recently, Tennessee State again when the Aristocrat of Bands became the first collegiate marching band to win a Grammy Award. That win for Best Gospel Album at the 2023 Grammy Awards was more than a trophy. It was a statement that HBCU band culture belongs not just in stadiums, but on the biggest stages in music. This wasn't a gimmick. It was excellence meeting opportunity. When you saw those bands on national TV, you saw Black brilliance choreographed to precision.

That influence didn't go unnoticed. By the early 1980s, HBCU bands were catching the attention of major brands. Florida A&M's Marching 100 appeared in a Welch's Grape Soda commercial—a rare national placement at the time. Around the same period, Grambling's band was featured in a Coca-Cola commercial, marking one of the earliest instances of a Black college band being used in a national ad campaign. It was unprecedented. In an era when mainstream media rarely gave HBCUs space, these moments signaled that corporate America was starting to recognize the cultural capital marching out of Black college stadiums every Saturday.

Today, students choose HBCUs specifically for the chance to march in these programs. Band directors aren't just instructors. They're recruiters, mentors, and cultural curators. And the bands themselves? They're a movement. They function like athletic programs, holding auditions, awarding scholarships, scouting high school talent, and holding grueling rehearsal schedules that mirror two-a-day football practices.

ZERO QUARTER AND FIFTH QUARTER

At HBCUs, the music starts before kickoff. Literally. While the players are warming up, the bands are already locked in— battling from across the field, challenging each other, daring the opposing side to match their energy. That's Zero Quarter.

Then there's the Fifth Quarter. The game ends, but nobody leaves. The bands turn the stadium into their own stage, trading songs like punches, each one louder and sharper than the last. It's a battle of pride, precision, and pure adrenaline. And if you know, you stay.

These two traditions, the Zero Quarter and the Fifth Quarter, aren't official. But they're sacred. Ask any fan, student, or alum, and they'll tell you: this is what makes HBCU football different.

It's not uncommon for fans to base their attendance around these moments. They'll tailgate early just to hear their band warm up. They'll hold off on leaving, even during a blowout, because the real showdown hasn't started yet. And it's not just the fans. Former band members—now alumni—return to games just to size up the next generation. Band rivalries are as real as the ones on the field. Sometimes more intense.

Classic Band Battles That Define the Culture

- Southern vs. Jackson State
- Florida A&M vs. Bethune-Cookman
- Texas Southern vs. Prairie View A&M
- North Carolina A&T vs. Norfolk State

- Alabama State vs. Alabama A&M

HALFTIME IS THE MAIN EVENT

At most schools, halftime is a break. At an HBCU game, it's the show.

This is when the band unleashes everything. Precision drills, dance routines, medleys of chart-toppers, and arrangements that get the crowd singing, shouting, and standing on their feet. Sometimes it's fun. Sometimes it's commentary. Sometimes it's flat-out pettiness. But always, it's powerful.

You don't just watch an HBCU halftime show, you experience it. And that experience has become just as recognizable as the programs themselves. If you see Southern's Human Jukebox or FAMU's Marching 100 take the field, you already know you're in for something unforgettable.

These performances are so layered that they could be broken into movements. You've got the opening fanfare, the theme of the week, the drumline feature, the dancers' spotlight, and the crowd-pleasing closer. And when we talk about the dancers, we're not talking about background support—we're talking about headliners in their own right. Squads like Southern's Dancing Dolls, Jackson State's J-Settes, and Alcorn State's Golden Girls are cultural institutions. Their precision, style, and choreography have shaped trends, inspired imitations, and earned their own spotlight in halftime lore. There's a reason these shows go viral—they're mini-productions built to entertain and inspire.

THE BUSINESS BEHIND THE BAND

Many HBCU bands are also tied directly to academic programs, especially in music education and performance studies. These programs don't just train musicians, they develop future music teachers, arrangers, and directors. For students, participating in the band can be both an artistic outlet and a pathway to a degree and career in education or the performing arts. This academic connection reinforces the fact that bands aren't just entertainment, they're part of the institutional mission.

Running an HBCU band isn't cheap. There's the cost of instruments, uniforms, buses, hotels, and food. And if the band's elite, multiply that by five.

That's why corporate partners like Honda and Pepsi have stepped in. The Honda Battle of the Bands and the National Battle of the Bands aren't just showcases—they're revenue drivers and recruiting tools. These events attract tens of thousands of spectators and give bands national exposure without needing a football game attached.

Some bands are even creating merch lines, streaming content, and finding ways to monetize their brand. Band directors today don't just need to know music but marketing, logistics, and leadership.

There are real stakes at play. Budget cuts have threatened band programs. But at some schools, the band is the face of the institution. Administrators know that. So do alumni. That's why there's increasing pressure to professionalize the operations—to find new ways to fund what's already priceless.

And travel? That's where the numbers start to really hit. Dr. Donovan Wells, longtime director of bands at Bethune-Cookman, broke it down plainly: a single trip to Alabama A&M, for a one-night stay, would cost the program nearly $88,000. "That's six buses, fuel surcharges, meals, and hotel rooms," he explained in a YouTube video interview with *The Ave|BCU*. "It's about $11,000 per day just to feed the band."

Bethune-Cookman's location on the Atlantic coast means it's further away from most SWAC schools than anyone else. In reality, that means long trips, high costs, and difficult choices. And while directors talk to one another, band travel isn't just a handshake agreement—it requires presidential and athletic department approval. These aren't just artistic decisions. They're institutional ones.

As Dr. Wells pointed out, the cost isn't just high for Bethune-Cookman. It's equally expensive for any SWAC band considering a trip to Daytona Beach, Florida. "No one has come to Daytona either," he said. "Because the same cost we would endure to go to, say, Alcorn, they would have to spend to come here." In other words, travel is a two-way burden. Geography and logistics aren't just hurdles; they're financial deal breakers.

WHERE MUSIC MEETS MOTIVATION

Talk to any football player who's suited up at an HBCU, and they'll tell you: the band matters. When that first note hits, when the drums start rolling, it lights a fire. It's a reminder of who you're playing for, and why it matters.

That energy can flip momentum. It can shake a visiting team. It can keep a crowd alive even when the scoreboard doesn't. A locked-in band makes the stadium feel electric.

In rivalry games, the band becomes part of the psychological battle. If your band is louder, cleaner, and more creative, it can feel like your school is winning, regardless of the score. The musicians in the stands become a 12th man of sorts. It's not just about being loud. It's about being heard.

Masters of the Sound: Legendary HBCU Band Directors

- **Dr. William P. Foster** – Florida A&M:
  Revolutionized show-style marching and created the internationally renowned Marching 100.
- **Conrad Hutchinson Jr.** – Grambling State: Raised

the bar for HBCU halftime performances and led the band to Super Bowl I.

- **Dr. Isaac Greggs** – Southern University: Built the Human Jukebox into one of the most iconic bands in the country.
- **Dowell Taylor** – Jackson State: Known for refining the Sonic Boom's sound and precision.
- **Dr. Donovan Wells** – Bethune-Cookman: Elevated BCU's band to national prominence through leadership, performance, and mentorship.
- **William H. Beathea** – Norfolk State: Modernized Spartan Legion while maintaining its traditional roots.
- **Dr. Reginald McDonald** – Tennessee State: Broke barriers by leading the Aristocrat of Bands to become the first collegiate marching band to win a Grammy.

FROM THE FIELD TO THE FEED

HBCU bands don't just own the field anymore. They own the timeline.

Viral halftime routines. Drum major entrances that rack up millions of views. TikToks, Reels, and Shorts that reach people who may never set foot on campus, but now know exactly what the culture looks and sounds like.

That reach has made bands one of the strongest brand tools an HBCU can have. Case in point: Tennessee State's Aristocrat of Bands made history when it won a Grammy in 2023 for Best Roots Gospel Album. That wasn't just a milestone—it was a mic drop for every HBCU band program. It proved that what happens in the stands can shape the music industry, not just half-time shows. They're drawing in recruits. They're creating emotional connections. They're turning performance into promotion.

And that visibility isn't accidental. Many bands now have dedicated content teams, students who shoot, edit, and post highlights in real time. Schools are building their marketing strategies around the performance units that already command attention.

It's not just music. It's marketing, momentum, and memory, all in one.

The game might bring fans in. But the band? The band brings them back.

HBCU bands don't just perform. They lead. They're part musical ensemble, part visual art, and part movement. They shape school identity. They move culture. They've helped define what Black excellence looks and sounds like. And whether they're rallying a crowd or going viral online, their impact stretches far beyond the field.

ELEVEN
THE HBCU ATHLETICS PLAYBOOK NEEDS A REWRITE

Not long ago, I had dinner with an HBCU football coach and some friends. It was a casual evening: friends talking shop, reflecting on the season, and catching up. But somewhere between appetizers and small talk, the conversation shifted.

He pulled out his phone and showed me pictures of his office. Then, photos of the team facility—walls chipped, ceiling tiles stained, and weight room equipment showing its age. What stood out wasn't just the condition of the space. It was the fact that he had no idea when, or even if, those things would be repaired. No timeline. No clear plan. Just quiet frustration and a reality far too many HBCU coaches know well.

That moment stuck with me because, as much pride as we carry, as much history as we honor, the current game demands more than tradition. When Eddie Robinson coached at Grambling, his biggest tools were belief and discipline. Today's coaches need compliance officers, NIL advisors, social media teams, and donor networks just to stay in the race.

The game hasn't just changed, it's been rewritten. And we're still playing on a field we didn't design.

HBCU sports have continuously operated on different

playing fields. One defined by resilience, creativity, and cultural pride. But in today's rapidly shifting landscape, tradition alone isn't enough to compete. From NIL to digital strategy, from outdated facilities to staff shortages, HBCUs are facing real, immediate challenges. And the pressure to evolve is coming from every direction.

This chapter unpacks those realities, the structural disadvantages, financial pressures, and operational gaps, and how HBCUs are addressing them. While the spotlight is growing, success in this new era won't be granted. It must be built.

NIL: A NEW ERA OF ATHLETE EMPOWERMENT

NIL isn't just shaping athlete decisions—it's influencing coaching moves, too.

Case in point: Donte' Jackson's decision to leave his position as Grambling's head men's basketball coach for the same role at Alabama A&M in April 2025. On the surface, it looked like a typical change of scenery. But listen closely to his reasoning, and the real story emerges.

"Kids want to be paid," Jackson said. "It's not as much about the other stuff like it was. The dynamic is changing."

Jackson made it clear he had no bad blood with Grambling, but the school's NIL strategy—or lack of one—played a role.

"They were doing a study on NIL," he said. "But I never got a clear answer on how it would work. It was all up in the air."

Meanwhile, Alabama A&M was, in his words, "doing some things when it comes to the resources they have and what they're trying to build up."

That clarity mattered. In today's game, coaches aren't just looking for tradition—they're looking for infrastructure. And if a coach, regardless of the sport, has to answer for wins and losses, it's not asking too much of the school that employs them to provide the tools needed to be successful.

Jackson's departure wasn't just about reuniting with Alabama A&M Athletics Director Paul Bryant (who hired him previously at Grambling) or starting fresh. It was about being in a place where the NIL game plan wasn't theoretical. It was real.

Culture gives us the edge, but structure keeps us in the fight. If we want to retain coaches, empower athletes, and compete beyond tradition, we have to build systems that match our influence.

We can't just inspire; we have to equip.

However, some HBCUs have already begun rewriting the NIL playbook.

At Morgan State University, the athletic department partnered with Teamworks and INFLCR to launch a campus-wide NIL Exchange. It's a digital platform that connects student-athletes with brands and businesses for paid opportunities. The system streamlines deal-making and includes education on branding, entrepreneurship, and compliance, giving Morgan athletes both access and understanding as they navigate this new landscape.

Howard University took a bold step in creating the Mecca Society, a donor-driven NIL collective launched in partnership with the myNILpay app. This platform allows fans and alumni to directly compensate athletes in real time. Howard athletes have already landed brand partnerships, including a historic team-wide deal between the women's basketball team and Black Girl Vitamins. The university's infrastructure ensures those deals come with support, not just exposure.

At Winston-Salem State, every student-athlete can sell co-branded merchandise through a partnership with Influxer while also receiving marketing and financial literacy training. For athletes at Division II schools, where national media attention is limited, that kind of income and education can be transformative.

Entire conferences are even getting involved.

In a historic decision announced in June 2025, the SWAC confirmed that all 12 of its member institutions will opt into the NCAA's multibillion-dollar antitrust settlement, clearing the way for direct athlete compensation beginning with the 2025–26 academic year. For context, this stems from the House v. NCAA case, which challenged the organization's long-standing restrictions on schools paying athletes directly. The result? A $2.8 billion agreement that doesn't just tweak the rules—it rewrites them.

Under the terms of the settlement, Division I schools can share up to $20 million annually with their athletes without affecting scholarships. That means HBCUs in the SWAC will now have the option to compensate athletes directly, not just through NIL endorsements but through actual revenue-sharing models. There are no more gray areas and no more hypotheticals. The amateurism era is officially coming to an end.

This is a watershed moment. It marks the first time an entire HBCU conference has taken a unified step toward structured pay-for-play. And while the money won't appear overnight, the implications are massive. The schools that plan, build, and adapt will thrive. The ones that wait will fall behind.

The question isn't just who's opting in.

It's who's ready for what comes next.

MEDIA RIGHTS AND VISIBILITY

In a media economy, visibility is currency. And too often, we're underpaid.

Platforms like ESPN+ and HBCU GO have moved the needle a bit. HBCU GO, now part of Byron Allen's Allen Media Group, broadcasts HBCU games across over-the-air channels and streaming platforms, reaching more than 70% of U.S. households.

Meanwhile, digital disruption has allowed schools and content creators to bypass traditional gatekeepers. During the Deion Sanders era, Jackson State expanded its digital footprint dramatically through in-house production and alumni-led coverage. Independent media outlets like HBCU Sports (hbcusport s.com) have proven that consistent, culturally informed coverage can rival or outperform traditional media outlets.

Even smaller schools and conferences are leaning into this space. The CIAA has secured ESPN coverage for its basketball tournament, and programs like North Carolina Central regularly post high-quality, in-house content on YouTube and social channels to engage fans and recruits alike.

It's not just about airtime. It's about authorship. We have to own our stories, produce at our level, and stop waiting for networks to validate our value. The spotlight is shifting, but it's on us to claim it.

FACILITIES AND INFRASTRUCTURE

Facilities don't win championships, but they help keep talent long enough to build one. And for too long, we've made magic without the resources to sustain it.

Take Tuskegee University, for example. One of the most historically successful HBCU athletic programs, Tuskegee, added stadium lighting to Cleve L. Abbott Memorial Alumni Stadium in 2024 for the first time. The upgrade wasn't just for night games; it created scheduling flexibility for late practices, reduced daytime heat risk, and allowed the field to be used for everything from classroom presentations to movie nights. The vision for lights actually dates back to 1926, first proposed by Coach Abbott himself. Nearly a century later, that vision has finally come to life.

Other institutions have relied on support from programs like Lowe's Campus Improvement Project or Home Depot's Retool

Your School to fund infrastructure upgrades. However, these efforts remain patchwork compared to the scale of the need.

If we want to win the long game, we must invest like we expect to be here, because we do.

CONFERENCE REALIGNMENT AND INSTITUTIONAL IDENTITY

Some HBCUs have responded to today's competitive pressures by reconsidering their place in the landscape, seeking growth in new conferences with new resources. Hampton, North Carolina A&T, Florida A&M, and Bethune-Cookman's recent moves to new athletic conferences have sparked a new wave of conversation: What's gained by leaving? And what's at risk?

For A&T, the jump from the MEAC to the Big South, and now the CAA, was about visibility and competition. The program initially gained more exposure, especially in track and field and baseball, but football attendance dropped, and the cultural footprint shifted. Hampton made a similar move to the CAA but struggled with crowd engagement and visibility, raising concerns about disconnecting from its traditional fan base. FAMU and BCU, in contrast, transitioned from the MEAC to the SWAC and saw their football brand explode, bolstered by large crowds, classic rivalries, and renewed media interest.

These different paths show that there's no one-size-fits-all answer. But the core question remains: What are we trading when we walk away from legacy, and is that trade-off worth it?

The question isn't just where we play but who we are when we get there. Growth is necessary, but not at the cost of identity. Every move must be strategic, not symbolic. What we're building isn't just a program—it's a legacy.

COMPLIANCE, STAFFING, AND ADMINISTRATIVE GAPS

You can't run a Division I program with a Division III back office. Passion has carried us far, but passion without capacity leads to burnout, not progress.

Across many HBCUs, athletic departments operate with skeleton crews. Sports information directors often manage all media relations, social content, website updates, and sometimes even serve as photographers. Coaches routinely juggle compliance tasks, academic oversight, recruiting, and operations. It's not uncommon for one person to wear four or five hats.

The result? Missed NIL opportunities, incomplete eligibility documentation, recruits slipping through the cracks, and programs falling behind, not because of a lack of talent, but because of a lack of bandwidth.

Some institutions have hired companies like Van Wagner to help with media rights and sponsorship support, but this doesn't always address the internal staffing challenges.

If we want sustainable success, we have to invest in people, not just job posts.

ATHLETE WELLNESS AND SUPPORT SERVICES

We ask a lot of our athletes. But too often, we don't have their back off the field. Mental health, emotional wellness, and recovery resources are often the first to get cut, or never built in the first place.

But that's slowly starting to change. In 2025, Edward Waters University launched the N.E.S.T. (Nurturing, Empowering & Supporting Tigers), a dedicated wellness room designed specifically for student-athletes. It was celebrated as the first of its kind among HBCUs. A powerful milestone, but also a reminder of how long these resources have been lacking.

According to a 2022 NCAA survey, student-athletes at under-resourced institutions report significantly higher rates of mental exhaustion, anxiety, and depression. And yet, most HBCUs still don't have full-time sports psychologists or designated wellness spaces.

Many of our athletes are first-generation college students balancing academic pressure, financial stress, and family expectations. If we want them to thrive, we have to support the whole athlete, not just the game-day version.

EMERGING SPORTS, FRAGILE SUPPORT

Expansion into new sports is often celebrated as a sign of growth and progress. However, expansion without infrastructure can just as easily result in a collapse.

That's the lesson many HBCUs are learning through the lens of women's gymnastics.

In 2022, Fisk University broke barriers as the first HBCU to launch a gymnastics program. Images of Black women tumbling, flipping, and sticking landings in maroon and gold lit up timelines and newsrooms. The program wasn't just historic; it was excellent. Fisk earned national rankings, a perfect 10 from standout Morgan Price, and respect from traditional NCAA programs. They proved that HBCUs could compete—and win—in spaces never built for them.

Talladega College followed in 2023 with its own gymnastics program. But by July 2024, the team was gone. Citing rising costs and lack of long-term support, the administration cut the program altogether. The decision left athletes like Kyrstin Johnson scrambling to find new homes. She eventually landed at Temple University. Others weren't so lucky.

In 2025, Morgan Price announced she would transfer to the

University of Arkansas, just weeks before Fisk confirmed plans to shut down its gymnastics program after the 2026 season. Three years after making history, the sport's future at Fisk was given an expiration date.

Today, Wilberforce University stands as the only HBCU with an active women's gymnastics program.

Launched in January 2025, Wilberforce's team is still in its early stages. It was built quickly with support from organizations like Brown Girls Do Gymnastics and the Isla® Foundation. The school even welcomed several displaced athletes from Talladega's roster. However, whether Wilberforce has the financial capacity and institutional infrastructure to carry this vision forward in the long term is still an open question.

That's the heart of the issue. It's not about whether HBCUs can launch new programs; it's about whether we can sustain them.

Visibility alone doesn't pay for coaches, facilities, or scholarships. Ambition must be matched by strategy. If we keep pioneering without building a foundation, these powerful firsts will fade into the background, reduced to headlines, hashtags, and footnotes.

Emerging sports can be more than experiments. They can be part of our evolution. But only if we invest accordingly.

DIGITAL STRATEGY AND FAN ENGAGEMENT

We don't lack content. We lack capacity. And yet, this is the battlefield where culture wins.

At Southern University, clips of the Human Jukebox Marching Band have gone viral on platforms like TikTok and Instagram, racking up millions of views and putting the school in front of new audiences. Other schools, like Prairie View A&M, have tapped into student talent. Communications majors help produce highlight reels, graphics, and social content, turning coursework into creative output that supports the athletic brand.

Athletes also benefit when schools invest in digital. A player with a steady flow of highlight clips, interviews, and media-ready photos is more likely to attract NIL interest. These assets build visibility, and visibility builds value.

The path forward isn't just about preserving tradition— it's about building the infrastructure to sustain it. Every NIL strategy implemented, every compliance officer hired, every wellness program launched moves us closer to a reality where our cultural advantages aren't undermined by structural disadvantages. The question isn't whether HBCUs can compete in this new land-scape, but whether we'll invest in the systems that make compe-tition sustainable.

TWELVE
LETTERS TO THE FUTURE

When I started covering HBCU sports, there was no blueprint for what I was trying to do. We weren't posting scores just to inform people; we were building something that reflected who we were as a culture, a community, and a platform.

Over the years, I've seen a lot change from message boards and fan forums to ESPN deals and NIL debates. However, one thing has remained true: HBCUs have always made a way out of no way. And HBCU athletics, in particular, has been one of the most resilient, underappreciated engines of Black excellence this country has ever seen.

This book was never just about stats or stories. It was about helping the next generation see what's been built and what still needs building.

So let me close with a few open letters to the people who will carry that work forward.

Dear Student-Athlete,

I know you feel the pressure.

You're balancing academics, expectations, sometimes a job, and now the added pressure of NIL and personal branding. It can feel like you're supposed to be an athlete, an influencer, and a spokesperson all at once.

But hear me clearly: You are enough, without the filters or the followers.

You are standing on the shoulders of athletes who never had your platform. Wilma Rudolph couldn't walk without braces as a child because of polio. But she went on to win three Olympic gold medals for Tennessee State and became the fastest woman in the world. To say she did more with less while at TSU is an understatement.

That's the kind of greatness your jersey represents. And that same spirit is still your foundation.

Learn your history. Ask your coaches about the legends who came before you. Speak up when something isn't right. And carry your legacy the way you carry your jersey—close to the chest, but visible for the world to see.

Dear Coach,

I've had the privilege of sitting with coaches over meals, in quiet offices, and in moments that didn't make the headlines. I've heard the stories, the frustrations, the hopes. I've seen what you carry. And I've seen how much of it goes unnoticed.

The truth is, you're asked to be a mentor, manager, recruiter, fundraiser, counselor, and PR rep, often with half the resources of your competitors. Oh, and you're still expected to win games.

And yet, you show up.

Not because it's easy. But because you know what's at stake.

Keep pushing, but don't do it in silence. Advocate for your athletes and for yourself. Demand the support you need, not just to win games, but to shape lives.

Coach Eddie Robinson didn't wait for conditions to be

perfect. He led with what he had and made the world respect it. That's still the blueprint.

Dear Administrator,

I've covered enough HBCU athletic departments to know what many of you are up against. You're working with lean budgets and high expectations. You know that athletics is a front-line for recruitment, visibility, and school pride—but often, you're making do with less.

But here's what I'll say as someone who's watched this space grow for decades: This isn't the time to play it safe. It's time to build.

Don't wait until something's broken to invest in it. NIL isn't a trend. It's a shift. Mental wellness isn't a checkbox. It's a necessity. Digital strategy isn't just marketing. It's storytelling.

You don't need to do everything at once. But you do need a plan. Build the systems now so your next generation of students and staff can thrive instead of survive.

Dear Alum,

You've been to the games. You've come back for Homecoming. You've repped your school in airports and group chats and on every casual Friday since graduation.

But pride by itself isn't enough.

I've seen what happens when alumni really show up; not just with posts and hashtags, but with purpose. When you give—even a little—it adds up. It might help cover a student media intern. It might help a team make a road trip. It might help keep someone in school.

Sometimes, just showing up to a random game (not just the classics) reminds these kids that somebody's watching. That somebody cares.

Legacy isn't just what you talk about. It's what you build.

Your school needs more than fans. It needs people who still give a damn—and prove it by what they give financially without asking for a seat at the table.

Dear Sponsor or Brand Leader,

If you've ever used a marching band clip in a campaign, spotlighted a "Divine Nine" moment, or co-opted the culture that was built at HBCUs, then know this: you're not just borrowing content. You're borrowing trust.

And trust comes with responsibility.

Invest in infrastructure, not just visibility. Support the schools, students, and storytellers who are shaping culture from the ground up, not just the ones trending this week.

When you fund an HBCU, you're not just sponsoring a game. You're anchoring your brand to a legacy of resilience, brilliance, and authenticity that can't be duplicated anywhere else.

Dear Future Storyteller,

You might be filming from the sidelines on your phone. You might be editing your first podcast or prepping your first campus interview. You might be wondering if what you're doing matters.

Let me assure you—it does.

When I started *HBCU Sports*, it wasn't about going viral. It was about showing our world on our terms. If you're doing that, you're already contributing to something bigger than content. You're contributing to continuity.

Tell the full story. Not just the scores. Not just the wins. The why. The how. The who. And when you do it, do it with integrity, not just reach.

Our stories don't need saving. They need to be documented.

. . .

To All of Us,

The system might need a new playbook.

But we don't.

We just need to run ours with conviction, clarity, and the courage to bet on ourselves.

We've never needed permission.

We've never waited for validation.

We've built, rebuilt, and reimagined—again and again.

And we'll keep doing it.

Because HBCU sports isn't just about what we've done.

It's about everything we're about to do.

ACKNOWLEDGMENTS

Like everything I've built through *HBCU Sports*, this book wouldn't exist without the people who walked with me through the journey.

First and foremost, I want to thank my lovely wife, Dionne, for her unwavering support. Woman, from the moment *HBCU Sports* was just an idea in my head, you have been my ride-or-die. You stood by me through every up and down, through late nights and long weekends, and even through the sacrifices that sometimes took time away from us. Words will never be enough to express the depth of my appreciation. Your belief in me made all of this possible. I love you more than words can express.

To my son, Malik, you might be the biggest Grambling fan I know who didn't even attend the school. Your passion and curiosity remind me daily why this work matters. Thank you for your constant encouragement and your genuine love for Black college culture.

To my son, Jamil, your decision to attend Grambling and continue the legacy means everything to me. Watching you take pride in our heritage is one of my proudest accomplishments as a father. My only hope is that future generations will carry that torch even further.

To Kendrick Marshall, my right hand and the senior editor of *HBCU Sports*, thank you for putting in the work that most people never see. Your commitment, vision, and consistency are a massive reason why this platform has become what it is today. I couldn't ask for a better teammate.

To Jarrett Hoffman and Chris Stevens, your voices, writing, and dedication have helped shape the identity of *HBCU Sports*. You both represent the future of this brand and as far as I'm concerned, you're family now. I appreciate everything you've contributed to this journey.

To the original supporters of the old SWAC Page message board—you laid the foundation. Your stories, debates, insights, and passion helped create the community that inspired this book. You were *HBCU Sports* before there was an *HBCU Sports*.

And finally, to the institution that raised me—Grambling State University. You are the greatest institution in the history of the universe, as far as I'm concerned. *"There's no doubt that we are the pride of the USA."*

CONNECT WITH HBCU SPORTS

HBCU Sports is the longest-running active digital media outlet dedicated exclusively to covering historically Black college and university athletics. Founded in 1997 as one of the first platforms of its kind, *HBCU Sports* helped establish a national voice for Black college sports in the digital era—long before social media and mainstream coverage gave HBCUs the spotlight they deserved.

The outlet has consistently delivered in-depth reporting, cultural commentary, and breaking news, all while pushing the conversation forward. From football and basketball to band culture and beyond, *HBCU Sports* remains a trusted source for fans, alumni, athletes, and supporters across the HBCU community.

———

Stay Connected With HBCU Sports

Website: hbcusports.com

youtube.com/@hbcusports

linkedin.com/company/hbcusports

instagram.com/hbcu_sports

facebook.com/realHBCUSports

x.com/HBCUSports

tiktok.com/@hbcusports

bsky.app/profile/hbcusports.bsky.social

threads.com/hbcu_sports

APPENDIX: THE HBCU DIRECTORY

This directory offers a snapshot of all 107 Historically Black Colleges and Universities across the United States. Each listing includes key details such as location, founding year, athletic affiliations, school colors, and mascot name. It's designed as a quick-reference guide for anyone wanting to know the schools that make up the HBCU family.

Alabama A&M University

- Location: Normal (Huntsville area), Alabama
- Founded: 1875
- Division & Conference: NCAA Division I FCS – Southwestern Athletic Conference (SWAC)
- Mascot: Bulldogs
- School Colors: Maroon and White

Alabama State University

- Location: Montgomery, Alabama
- Founded: 1867

- Division & Conference: NCAA Division I FCS – Southwestern Athletic Conference (SWAC)
- Mascot: Hornets
- School Colors: Black and Old Gold

Albany State University

- Location: Albany, Georgia
- Founded: 1903
- Division & Conference: NCAA Division II – Southern Intercollegiate Athletic Conference (SIAC)
- Mascot: Golden Rams
- School Colors: Royal Blue and Old Gold

Alcorn State University

- Location: Lorman, Mississippi
- Founded: 1871
- Division & Conference: NCAA Division I FCS – Southwestern Athletic Conference (SWAC)
- Mascot: Braves
- School Colors: Purple and Gold

Allen University

- Location: Columbia, South Carolina
- Founded: 1870
- Division & Conference: NCAA Division II – Southern Intercollegiate Athletic Conference (SIAC)
- Mascot: Yellow Jackets
- School Colors: Blue and White

American Baptist College

- Location: Nashville, Tennessee
- Founded: 1924
- Division & Conference: NAIA – National Christian College Athletic Association (NCCAA)
- Mascot: Sabers
- School Colors: Blue and White

Arkansas Baptist College

- Location: Little Rock, Arkansas
- Founded: 1884
- Division & Conference: NAIA – Independent
- Mascot: Buffaloes
- School Colors: Royal Blue and White

Barber-Scotia College

- Location: Concord, North Carolina
- Founded: 1867
- Division & Conference: New South Athletic Conference (NSAC)
- Mascot: Sabers
- School Colors: Royal Blue and Gray

Benedict College

- Location: Columbia, South Carolina
- Founded: 1870
- Division & Conference: NCAA Division II – Southern Intercollegiate Athletic Conference (SIAC)
- Mascot: Tigers
- School Colors: Purple and Gold

Bennett College

- Location: Greensboro, North Carolina
- Founded: 1873
- Division & Conference: NCAA Division III – Independent
- Mascot: Belles
- School Colors: Royal Blue and White

Bethune-Cookman University

- Location: Daytona Beach, Florida
- Founded: 1904
- Division & Conference: NCAA Division I FCS – Southwestern Athletic Conference (SWAC)
- Mascot: Wildcats
- School Colors: Maroon and Gold

Bishop State Community College

- Location: Mobile, Alabama
- Founded: 1927
- Division & Conference: NJCAA – Region 22
- Mascot: Wildcats
- School Colors: Green and Gold

Bluefield State University

- Location: Bluefield, West Virginia
- Founded: 1895
- Division & Conference: NCAA Division II – Central Intercollegiate Athletic Association (CIAA)
- Mascot: Big Blue
- School Colors: Royal Blue and Gold

Bowie State University

- Location: Bowie, Maryland
- Founded: 1865
- Division & Conference: NCAA Division II – CIAA
- Mascot: Bulldogs
- School Colors: Black and Gold

Carver College

- Location: Atlanta, Georgia
- Founded: 1943
- Division & Conference: NCCAA – South Region
- Mascot: Cougars
- School Colors: Royal Blue and White

Central State University

- Location: Wilberforce, Ohio
- Founded: 1887
- Division & Conference: NCAA Division II – SIAC
- Mascot: Marauders
- School Colors: Maroon and Gold

Cheyney University of Pennsylvania

- Location: Cheyney, Pennsylvania
- Founded: 1837
- Division & Conference: NCAA Division II – Independent (Formerly CIAA)
- Mascot: Wolves
- School Colors: Royal Blue and White

Claflin University

- Location: Orangeburg, South Carolina

- Founded: 1869
- Division & Conference: NCAA Division II – Central Intercollegiate Athletic Association (CIAA)
- Mascot: Panthers
- School Colors: Orange and Maroon

Clark Atlanta University

- Location: Atlanta, Georgia
- Founded: 1988 (by the consolidation of Clark College, 1869, and Atlanta University, 1865)
- Division & Conference: NCAA Division II – Southern Intercollegiate Athletic Conference (SIAC)
- Mascot: Panthers
- School Colors: Red and Black

Clinton College

- Location: Rock Hill, South Carolina
- Founded: 1894
- Division & Conference: NCCAA – Independent
- Mascot: Golden Bears
- School Colors: Royal Blue and Gold

Coahoma Community College

- Location: Clarksdale, Mississippi
- Founded: 1949
- Division & Conference: NJCAA – Region 23
- Mascot: Tigers
- School Colors: Maroon and White

Coppin State University

- Location: Baltimore, Maryland
- Founded: 1900
- Division & Conference: NCAA Division I – Mid-Eastern Athletic Conference (MEAC)
- Mascot: Eagles
- School Colors: Royal Blue and Gold

Delaware State University

- Location: Dover, Delaware
- Founded: 1891
- Division & Conference: NCAA Division I FCS – MEAC
- Mascot: Hornets
- School Colors: Red and Columbia Blue

Denmark Technical College

- Location: Denmark, South Carolina
- Founded: 1947
- Division & Conference: NJCAA – Region 10
- Mascot: Panthers
- School Colors: Blue and White

Dillard University

- Location: New Orleans, Louisiana
- Founded: 1869
- Division & Conference: NAIA – HBCU Athletic Conference (HBCUAC)
- Mascot: Bleu Devils
- School Colors: Royal Blue and White

Drake State Community and Technical College

- Location: Huntsville, Alabama
- Founded: 1961
- Division & Conference: NJCAA – Region 22
- Mascot: Eagles
- School Colors: Green and Gold

Edward Waters University

- Location: Jacksonville, Florida
- Founded: 1866
- Division & Conference: NCAA Division II – SIAC
- Mascot: Tigers
- School Colors: Purple and Orange

Elizabeth City State University

- Location: Elizabeth City, North Carolina
- Founded: 1891
- Division & Conference: NCAA Division II – CIAA
- Mascot: Vikings
- School Colors: Royal Blue and White

Fayetteville State University

- Location: Fayetteville, North Carolina
- Founded: 1867
- Division & Conference: NCAA Division II – CIAA
- Mascot: Broncos
- School Colors: Royal Blue and White

Fisk University

- Location: Nashville, Tennessee
- Founded: 1866

- Division & Conference: NAIA – HBCU Athletic Conference (HBCUAC)
- Mascot: Bulldogs
- School Colors: Gold and Blue

Florida A&M University

- Location: Tallahassee, Florida
- Founded: 1887
- Division & Conference: NCAA Division I FCS – Southwestern Athletic Conference (SWAC)
- Mascot: Rattlers
- School Colors: Orange and Green

Florida Memorial University

- Location: Miami Gardens, Florida
- Founded: 1879
- Division & Conference: NAIA – Sun Conference
- Mascot: Lions
- School Colors: Royal Blue and Orange

Fort Valley State University

- Location: Fort Valley, Georgia
- Founded: 1895
- Division & Conference: NCAA Division II – SIAC
- Mascot: Wildcats
- School Colors: Blue and Gold

Gadsden State Community College

- Location: Gadsden, Alabama
- Founded: 1925 (Valley Street Campus added 1960s)

- Division & Conference: NJCAA – Region 22
- Mascot: Cardinals
- School Colors: Red and White

Grambling State University

- Location: Grambling, Louisiana
- Founded: 1901
- Division & Conference: NCAA Division I FCS – SWAC
- Mascot: Tigers
- School Colors: Black and Gold

Hampton University

- Location: Hampton, Virginia
- Founded: 1868
- Division & Conference: NCAA Division I FCS – Coastal Athletic Association (CAA)
- Mascot: Pirates
- School Colors: Reflex Blue and White

Harris-Stowe State University

- Location: St. Louis, Missouri
- Founded: 1857
- Division & Conference: NAIA – American Midwest Conference
- Mascot: Hornets
- School Colors: Brown and Gold

Hinds Community College – Utica Campus

- Location: Utica, Mississippi

- Founded: 1903
- Division & Conference: NJCAA – Region 23
- Mascot: Bulldogs
- School Colors: Maroon and White

Howard University

- Location: Washington, D.C.
- Founded: 1867
- Division & Conference: NCAA Division I FCS –
  Mid-Eastern Athletic Conference (MEAC)
- Mascot: Bison
- School Colors: Blue, White, and Red

Huston-Tillotson University

- Location: Austin, Texas
- Founded: 1875
- Division & Conference: NAIA – HBCU Athletic
  Conference (HBCUAC)
- Mascot: Rams
- School Colors: Maroon and Gold

Interdenominational Theological Center (ITC)

- Location: Atlanta, Georgia
- Founded: 1958
- Division & Conference: Not applicable (Graduate
  theological consortium)
- Mascot: N/A
- School Colors: Maroon and White

Jackson State University

- Location: Jackson, Mississippi
- Founded: 1877
- Division & Conference: NCAA Division I FCS – Southwestern Athletic Conference (SWAC)
- Mascot: Tigers
- School Colors: Navy Blue and White

Jarvis Christian University

- Location: Hawkins, Texas
- Founded: 1912
- Division & Conference: NAIA – Red River Athletic Conference
- Mascot: Bulldogs
- School Colors: Royal Blue and White

Johnson C. Smith University

- Location: Charlotte, North Carolina
- Founded: 1867
- Division & Conference: NCAA Division II – Central Intercollegiate Athletic Association (CIAA)
- Mascot: Golden Bulls
- School Colors: Blue and Gold

Kentucky State University

- Location: Frankfort, Kentucky
- Founded: 1886
- Division & Conference: NCAA Division II – Southern Intercollegiate Athletic Conference (SIAC)
- Mascot: Thorobreds
- School Colors: Green and Gold

Knoxville College

- Location: Knoxville, Tennessee
- Founded: 1875
- Division & Conference: Not applicable
- Mascot: Bulldogs
- School Colors: Garnet and Blue

Lane College

- Location: Jackson, Tennessee
- Founded: 1882
- Division & Conference: NCAA Division II –
  Southern Intercollegiate Athletic Conference (SIAC)
- Mascot: Dragons
- School Colors: Maroon and White

Langston University

- Location: Langston, Oklahoma
- Founded: 1897
- Division & Conference: NAIA – Sooner Athletic
  Conference
- Mascot: Lions
- School Colors: Blue and Orange

Lawson State Community College

- Location: Birmingham, Alabama
- Founded: 1949
- Division & Conference: NJCAA – Region 22
- Mascot: Cougars
- School Colors: Royal Blue and Gold

LeMoyne-Owen College

- Location: Memphis, Tennessee
- Founded: 1862
- Division & Conference: NCAA Division II – SIAC
- Mascot: Magicians
- School Colors: Purple and Gold

Lincoln University (Missouri)

- Location: Jefferson City, Missouri
- Founded: 1866
- Division & Conference: NCAA Division II – Great Lakes Valley Conference (GLVC)
- Mascot: Blue Tigers
- School Colors: Blue and White

Lincoln University (Pennsylvania)

- Location: Lincoln University, Pennsylvania
- Founded: 1854
- Division & Conference: NCAA Division II – CIAA
- Mascot: Lions
- School Colors: Orange and Blue

Livingstone College

- Location: Salisbury, North Carolina
- Founded: 1879
- Division & Conference: NCAA Division II – CIAA
- Mascot: Blue Bears
- School Colors: Blue and White

Meharry Medical College

- Location: Nashville, Tennessee
- Founded: 1876
- Division & Conference: Graduate/Health Sciences – No athletics
- Mascot: None
- School Colors: Burgundy and White

Miles College

- Location: Fairfield, Alabama
- Founded: 1898
- Division & Conference: NCAA Division II – SIAC
- Mascot: Golden Bears
- School Colors: Purple and Gold

Miles School of Law

- Location: Fairfield, Alabama
- Founded: 1974
- Division & Conference: No athletics
- Mascot: N/A
- School Colors: Purple and Gold

Mississippi Valley State University

- Location: Itta Bena, Mississippi
- Founded: 1950
- Division & Conference: NCAA Division I FCS – SWAC
- Mascot: Delta Devils
- School Colors: Forest Green and White

Morehouse College

- Location: Atlanta, Georgia
- Founded: 1867
- Division & Conference: NCAA Division II – SIAC
- Mascot: Maroon Tigers
- School Colors: Maroon and White

Morehouse School of Medicine

- Location: Atlanta, Georgia
- Founded: 1975
- Division & Conference: Graduate/Health Sciences – No athletics
- Mascot: None
- School Colors: Maroon and White

Morgan State University

- Location: Baltimore, Maryland
- Founded: 1867
- Division & Conference: NCAA Division I FCS – MEAC
- Mascot: Bears
- School Colors: Orange and Blue

Morris Brown College

- Location: Atlanta, Georgia
- Founded: 1881
- Division & Conference: NAIA – Independent
- Mascot: Wolverines
- School Colors: Purple and Black

Morris College

- Location: Sumter, South Carolina
- Founded: 1908
- Division & Conference: NAIA – Independent
- Mascot: Hornets
- School Colors: Royal Blue and Gold

Norfolk State University

- Location: Norfolk, Virginia
- Founded: 1935
- Division & Conference: NCAA Division I FCS – MEAC
- Mascot: Spartans
- School Colors: Green and Gold

North Carolina A&T State University

- Location: Greensboro, North Carolina
- Founded: 1891
- Division & Conference: NCAA Division I FCS – Coastal Athletic Association (CAA)
- Mascot: Aggies
- School Colors: Blue and Gold

North Carolina Central University

- Location: Durham, North Carolina
- Founded: 1910
- Division & Conference: NCAA Division I FCS – MEAC
- Mascot: Eagles
- School Colors: Maroon and Gray

Oakwood University

- Location: Huntsville, Alabama
- Founded: 1896
- Division & Conference: NAIA – HBCU Athletic Conference (HBCUAC)
- Mascot: Ambassadors
- School Colors: Navy Blue and Gold

Paine College

- Location: Augusta, Georgia
- Founded: 1882
- Division & Conference: NCCAA – Independent (formerly SIAC)
- Mascot: Lions
- School Colors: Purple and White

Paul Quinn College

- Location: Dallas, Texas
- Founded: 1872
- Division & Conference: NAIA – HBCU Athletic Conference (HBCUAC)
- Mascot: Tigers
- School Colors: Royal Blue and Gold

Philander Smith University

- Location: Little Rock, Arkansas
- Founded: 1877
- Division & Conference: NAIA – HBCU Athletic Conference (HBCUAC)
- Mascot: Panthers
- School Colors: Green and Gold

Prairie View A&M University

- Location: Prairie View, Texas
- Founded: 1876
- Division & Conference: NCAA Division I FCS – SWAC
- Mascot: Panthers
- School Colors: Purple and Gold

Rust College

- Location: Holly Springs, Mississippi
- Founded: 1866
- Division & Conference: NAIA – HBCU Athletic Conference (HBCUAC)
- Mascot: Bearcats
- School Colors: Royal Blue and White

Saint Augustine's University

- Location: Raleigh, North Carolina
- Founded: 1867
- Division & Conference: NCAA Division II – CIAA
- Mascot: Falcons
- School Colors: Royal Blue and White

Savannah State University

- Location: Savannah, Georgia
- Founded: 1890
- Division & Conference: NCAA Division II – SIAC
- Mascot: Tigers
- School Colors: Burnt Orange and Navy Blue

Selma University

- Location: Selma, Alabama
- Founded: 1878
- Division & Conference: NCCAA – Independent
- Mascot: Bulldogs
- School Colors: Blue and White

Shaw University

- Location: Raleigh, North Carolina
- Founded: 1865
- Division & Conference: NCAA Division II – CIAA
- Mascot: Bears
- School Colors: Garnet and White

Shelton State Community College

- Location: Tuscaloosa, Alabama
- Founded: 1952
- Division & Conference: NJCAA – Region 22
- Mascot: Buccaneers
- School Colors: Green and White

Shorter College

- Location: North Little Rock, Arkansas
- Founded: 1886
- Division & Conference: NJCAA – Independent
- Mascot: Bulldogs
- School Colors: Blue and White

Simmons College of Kentucky

- Location: Louisville, Kentucky
- Founded: 1879
- Division & Conference: NAIA – Mid-South Conference
- Mascot: Falcons
- School Colors: Blue and Gold

Southern University at New Orleans

- Location: New Orleans, Louisiana
- Founded: 1956
- Division & Conference: NAIA – HBCU Athletic Conference (HBCUAC)
- Mascot: Knights
- School Colors: Blue and Gold

Southern University at Shreveport

- Location: Shreveport, Louisiana
- Founded: 1967
- Division & Conference: NJCAA – Region 23
- Mascot: Jaguars
- School Colors: Blue and Gold

Southern University Law Center

- Location: Baton Rouge, Louisiana
- Founded: 1947
- Division & Conference: Graduate/Law – No athletics
- Mascot: None
- School Colors: Blue and Gold

Southern University and A&M College

- Location: Baton Rouge, Louisiana
- Founded: 1880
- Division & Conference: NCAA Division I FCS –
  SWAC
- Mascot: Jaguars
- School Colors: Columbia Blue and Gold

South Carolina State University

- Location: Orangeburg, South Carolina
- Founded: 1896
- Division & Conference: NCAA Division I FCS –
  MEAC
- Mascot: Bulldogs
- School Colors: Garnet and Blue

Southwestern Christian College

- Location: Terrell, Texas
- Founded: 1948
- Division & Conference: NJCAA – Region 5
- Mascot: Rams
- School Colors: Blue and White

Spelman College

- Location: Atlanta, Georgia
- Founded: 1881
- Division & Conference: No intercollegiate athletics
  program
- Mascot: Jaguars
- School Colors: Columbia Blue and White

St. Philip's College

- Location: San Antonio, Texas
- Founded: 1898
- Division & Conference: NJCAA – Region 14
- Mascot: Tigers
- School Colors: Royal Blue and White

Stillman College

- Location: Tuscaloosa, Alabama
- Founded: 1876
- Division & Conference: NAIA – Southern States Athletic Conference (SSAC)
- Mascot: Tigers
- School Colors: Navy Blue and Vegas Gold

Talladega College

- Location: Talladega, Alabama
- Founded: 1867
- Division & Conference: NAIA – Southern States Athletic Conference (SSAC)
- Mascot: Tornadoes
- School Colors: Crimson and Old Gold

Tennessee State University

- Location: Nashville, Tennessee
- Founded: 1912
- Division & Conference: NCAA Division I FCS – Ohio Valley Conference (OVC)
- Mascot: Tigers
- School Colors: Royal Blue and White

Texas College

- Location: Tyler, Texas
- Founded: 1894
- Division & Conference: NAIA – Sooner Athletic Conference (SAC)
- Mascot: Steers
- School Colors: Purple and Gold

Texas Southern University

- Location: Houston, Texas
- Founded: 1927
- Division & Conference: NCAA Division I FCS – SWAC
- Mascot: Tigers
- School Colors: Maroon and Gray

Tougaloo College

- Location: Tougaloo, Mississippi
- Founded: 1869
- Division & Conference: NAIA – HBCU Athletic Conference (HBCUAC)
- Mascot: Bulldogs
- School Colors: Royal Blue and Scarlet

Trenholm State Community College

- Location: Montgomery, Alabama
- Founded: 1963
- Division & Conference: NJCAA – Region 22
- Mascot: Tigers
- School Colors: Burgundy and Gray

Tuskegee University

- Location: Tuskegee, Alabama
- Founded: 1881
- Division & Conference: NCAA Division II – SIAC
- Mascot: Golden Tigers
- School Colors: Crimson and Old Gold

University of Arkansas at Pine Bluff

- Location: Pine Bluff, Arkansas
- Founded: 1873
- Division & Conference: NCAA Division I FCS – SWAC
- Mascot: Golden Lions
- School Colors: Black and Gold

University of Maryland Eastern Shore

- Location: Princess Anne, Maryland
- Founded: 1886
- Division & Conference: NCAA Division I – MEAC
- Mascot: Hawks
- School Colors: Maroon and Gray

University of the District of Columbia

- Location: Washington, D.C.
- Founded: 1851
- Division & Conference: NCAA Division II – East Coast Conference (ECC)
- Mascot: Firebirds
- School Colors: Red and Gold

University of the Virgin Islands

- Location: Charlotte Amalie, St. Thomas, U.S. Virgin Islands
- Founded: 1962
- Division & Conference: NAIA – HBCU Athletic Conference (HBCUAC)
- Mascot: Buccaneers
- School Colors: Blue, White, and Gold

Virginia State University

- Location: Petersburg, Virginia
- Founded: 1882
- Division & Conference: NCAA Division II – CIAA
- Mascot: Trojans
- School Colors: Orange and Blue

Virginia Union University

- Location: Richmond, Virginia
- Founded: 1865
- Division & Conference: NCAA Division II – CIAA
- Mascot: Panthers
- School Colors: Maroon and Steel Gray

Virginia University of Lynchburg

- Location: Lynchburg, Virginia
- Founded: 1886
- Division & Conference: NCCAA – Independent
- Mascot: Dragons
- School Colors: Purple and White

Voorhees University

- Location: Denmark, South Carolina
- Founded: 1897
- Division & Conference: NAIA – Continental Athletic Conference
- Mascot: Tigers
- School Colors: Royal Blue and White

West Virginia State University

- Location: Institute, West Virginia
- Founded: 1891
- Division & Conference: NCAA Division II – Mountain East Conference
- Mascot: Yellow Jackets
- School Colors: Black and Gold

Wilberforce University

- Location: Wilberforce, Ohio
- Founded: 1856
- Division & Conference: NAIA – Mid-South Conference
- Mascot: Bulldogs
- School Colors: Forest Green and Old Gold

Wiley University

- Location: Marshall, Texas
- Founded: 1873
- Division & Conference: NAIA – HBCU Athletic Conference (HBCUAC)
- Mascot: Wildcats
- School Colors: Maroon and White

Winston-Salem State University

- Location: Winston-Salem, North Carolina
- Founded: 1892
- Division & Conference: NCAA Division II – CIAA
- Mascot: Rams
- School Colors: Red and White

Xavier University of Louisiana

- Location: New Orleans, Louisiana
- Founded: 1925
- Division & Conference: NAIA – Red River Athletic Conference
- Mascot: Gold Rush (men), Gold Nuggets (women)
- School Colors: Gold and White

ENDNOTES

Introduction

1 *HBCU Sports*, "Sources: Jackson State to name Deion Sanders new head football coach," September 17, 2020, https://hbcusports.com/football/deion-sanders-jackson-state/.

Chapter 1

1 Higher Education Act of 1965, Title III, Part B—formally defining HBCUs as institutions established before 1964 with the primary mission of educating Black Americans. U.S. Department of Education, "Title III Part B, Strengthening Historically Black Colleges and Universities Program," accessed June 2025, https://www.ed.gov/grants-and-programs/grants-higher-education/grants-hbcus/title-iii-part-b-strengthening-historically-black-colleges-and-universities-program.

2 Encyclopaedia Britannica, s.v. "Historically Black Colleges and Universities (HBCUs)," accessed June 2025, https://www.britannica.com/topic/historically-black-colleges-and-universities.

3 Wikipedia, s.v. "Historically black colleges and universities," last revised June 2025, https://en.wikipedia.org/wiki/Historically_black_colleges_and_universities.

4 Cheyney University was founded on February 25, 1837, through a bequest from Richard Humphreys, establishing it as the nation's first HBCU. Encyclopaedia Britannica, s.v. "Cheyney University of Pennsylvania," accessed June 2025, https://www.britannica.com/topic/Cheyney-University-of-Pennsylvania.

5 Lincoln University received its charter on April 29, 1854, becoming the first degree-granting HBCU. History.com, "First HBCU, Lincoln University, chartered," February 15, 2024, https://www.history.com/this-day-in-history/lincoln-university-first-hbcu-chartered.

6 Most HBCUs were founded during the Reconstruction era (1865–1877) in response to post–Civil War exclusion. Wikipedia, s.v. "Historically black colleges and universities," https://en.wikipedia.org/wiki/Historically_black_colleges_and_universities.

7 Early HBCUs were established to prepare Black students for careers in teaching, trade, health, engineering, the arts, activism, and athletics. Encyclopaedia Britannica, s.v. "HBCUs," https://www.britannica.com/topic/historically-black-colleges-and-universities.

8 Predominantly white institutions (PWIs) systematically denied Black students admission, prompting the founding of HBCUs. Encyclopaedia Britannica; Wikipedia, s.v. "Historically black colleges and universities," https://en.wiki pedia.org/wiki/Historically_black_colleges_and_universities.

9 As Brian Bridges observed, "HBCUs make up only three percent of the country's colleges and universities, but enroll 10 percent of all African American students and produce almost 20 percent of all African American graduates." United Negro College Fund, "The Numbers Don't Lie: HBCUs Are Changing the College Landscape," February 8, 2022, https://uncf.org/the-lat est/the-numbers-dont-lie-hbcus-are-changing-the-college-landscape.

10 HBCU athletic programs originated as platforms of resistance and cultural affirmation when mainstream sports outlets ignored Black athletes. Encyclopaedia Britannica; Wikipedia, s.v. "Historically black colleges and universities," https://en.wikipedia.org/wiki/Historically_black_colleges_and_universities.

11 Athletes from HBCUs went on to help integrate professional sports—such as the NFL, NBA, MLB—and Olympic teams, reshaping the racial landscape in U.S. athletics. Encyclopaedia Britannica; Wikipedia, s.v. "Historically black colleges and universities," https://en.wikipedia.org/wiki/Historically_black_ colleges_and_universities.

Chapter 2

1 The first football game between HBCUs occurred December 27, 1892, when Livingstone College faced Biddle University (now Johnson C. Smith University) at Livingstone's snowy Salisbury, NC campus. Wikipedia, s.v. "1892 Biddle vs. Livingstone football game," last revised June 2025, https://en.wiki pedia.org/wiki/1892_Biddle_vs._Livingstone_football_game.

2 Biddle won 4–0 (or 5–0 per some sources); a touchdown counted four points then; the frozen cow pasture field and shoes with cleats illustrated student resourcefulness. "HBCU Football History," *Celebration Bowl*, accessed June 2025, https://www.thecelebrationbowl.com/history/hbcu-football-history/; "The First HBCU College Football Game in America Is Played," *African American Registry*, https://aaregistry.org/story/first-black-college-football-game-played/.

3 The Colored Intercollegiate Athletic Association (CIAA) was founded in 1912 with charter members Hampton, Howard, Lincoln (PA), Shaw, and Virginia Union. Encyclopaedia Britannica, s.v. "Central Intercollegiate Athletic Association," accessed June 2025, https://www.britannica.com/topic/Central-Inter collegiate-Athletic-Association.

4 The Southern Intercollegiate Athletic Conference (SIAC) began in 1913 with founding members including Alabama State, Clark Atlanta, Fisk, Jackson

State, Morris Brown, Morehouse, Talladega, and Tuskegee. *SIAC Official Archives*, accessed June 2025.

5 The Southwestern Athletic Conference (SWAC) launched in 1920 with Bishop College, Paul Quinn, Prairie View A&M, Texas College, and Wiley College. *SWAC Historical Overview*, accessed June 2025.

6 The Mid-Eastern Athletic Conference (MEAC) broke from CIAA in 1970, becoming Division I with charter members Delaware State, Howard, UMES, Morgan State, NC A&T, NC Central, and South Carolina State. *MEAC History*, accessed June 2025.

7 Ed Temple coached Tennessee State's Tigerbelles to 40 Olympians and 23 Olympic medals (13 gold, 6 silver, 4 bronze). "Ed Temple," *U.S. Olympic & Paralympic Museum*, accessed June 2025, https://usopm.org/ed-temple/; "Legendary Tennessee State Coach Ed Temple Dies," *Andscape*, accessed June 2025, https://andscape.com/features/legendary-tennessee-state-coach-coach-ed-temple-dies/.

8 Under Coach Jake Gaither, Florida A&M football rose to national prominence in the mid-20th century. *Florida A&M Football History*, accessed June 2025.

9 Coach Eddie Robinson of Grambling State sent over 200 players to the NFL during his tenure. *Grambling Athletics Department Records*, accessed June 2025.

10 Southern University's Rickie Weeks was selected No. 2 overall in the 2003 MLB Draft. *MLB Draft History*, accessed June 2025.

11 Winston-Salem State's Earl "The Pearl" Monroe led his team to the 1967 NCAA Division II title before NBA stardom. *NCAA Archives*, accessed June 2025.

12 Vivian Stringer coached Cheyney State's women's basketball team to the 1982 NCAA Final Four. *NCAA Women's Final Four Records*, accessed June 2025.

13 Black-owned newspapers—the *Pittsburgh Courier*, *Chicago Defender*, and *Baltimore Afro-American*—provided consistent coverage of HBCU athletics overlooked by mainstream media. *Black Press Archives*, accessed June 2025.

14 Collie J. Nicholson, Grambling State's SID from 1948–1978, organized games at Yankee Stadium and Tokyo, and helped found the Bayou Classic. "SID History," *Grambling State Athletics*, accessed June 2025.

15 Integration in the 1960s–70s led PWIs to recruit Black athletes, triggering talent and revenue loss at HBCUs. *Journal of Sports Sociology* 45, no. 2 (2020).

16 In 2020, Makur Maker and sisters Mikayla & Mariah Allison chose Howard University; Jackson State hired Deion Sanders in 2020, who left for Colorado in 2023—shifting media focus from HBCUs to Sanders. *ESPN*, *The Athletic*, various articles (2020–2023).

17 The first documented HBCU baseball game was played in 1887 between

Southern University and Straight University in New Orleans. "The History of HBCU Baseball," *Black College Nines*, accessed June 2025, https://blackcol legenines.com.

18 Southern University was founded in 1880 and originally located on Magazine Street in New Orleans; Straight University was founded in 1869 and later merged into Dillard University. "Southern University and A&M College," *BlackPast.org*, accessed June 2025, https://www.blackpast.org; Wikipedia, s.v. "Straight University," last modified June 2025, https://en.wikipedia.org/ wiki/Straight_University.

19 Due to the lack of contemporary documentation, specifics about the 1887 game's score and outcome remain unknown, but baseball historians widely accept it as the earliest documented intercollegiate game between Black colleges. Jay Sokol, *Black College Nines: The History of HBCU Baseball*, SABR Research, accessed June 2025.

Chapter 3

1 The Southwestern Athletic Conference (SWAC) was founded in 1920 in Houston by athletic officials from six Texas HBCUs to formalize competition and visibility for Black college athletics. *Southwestern Athletic Conference*, "Founded in 1920…six colleges," accessed June 2025, https://swac.org/ sports/2020/5/21/GEN_0521200905.aspx; *Wikipedia*, s.v. "Southwestern Athletic Conference," last revised June 2025, https://en.wikipedia.org/wiki/ Southwestern_Athletic_Conference.

2 SWAC's charter members were Bishop College, Paul Quinn College, Prairie View A&M, Texas College, Wiley College, and Huston–Tillotson. *Wikipedia*, s.v. "Southwestern Athletic Conference," https://en.wikipedia.org/wiki/South western_Athletic_Conference; *Bhamwiki*, "Southwestern Athletic Confer-ence," accessed June 2025, https://www.bhamwiki.com/w/ Southwestern_Athletic_Conference.

3 In 2021, Florida A&M and Bethune–Cookman left the MEAC to join the SWAC's East Division, expanding its geographic footprint. *SWAC news*, "Division realignment with additions of Florida A&M and Bethune–Cook-man," accessed June 2025.

4 The Mid-Eastern Athletic Conference (MEAC) was founded in 1970 after seven schools separated from the CIAA to establish a Division I presence on the East Coast. *MEAC History*, accessed June 2025.

5 The CIAA, originally the Colored Intercollegiate Athletic Association, was established in 1912 and is the oldest HBCU athletic conference. *Ency-clopaedia Britannica*, s.v. "Central Intercollegiate Athletic Association," accessed June 2025, https://www.britannica.com/topic/Central-Intercolle giate-Athletic-Association.

6 The SIAC was founded in 1913 in Atlanta to support organized athletic compe-

tition among Southeastern HBCUs, including Alabama State, Tuskegee, and Morehouse. *SIAC archives*, accessed June 2025.

7 In March 2024, GCAC Commissioner Dr. Kiki Baker Barnes announced the rebrand to the "HBCU Athletic Conference," effective July 1, as a strategic move to solidify the conference's identity and visibility. *Bold move: GCAC commissioner reveals 'HBCU Athletic Conference' rebrand, HBCU Sports,* March 10, 2024, https://hbcusports.com/2024/03/10/bold-move-gcac-commis sioner-reveals-hbcu-athletic-conference-rebrand/.

8 The HBCUAC was originally founded in 1981 as the Gulf Coast Athletic Conference. *Wikipedia*, s.v. "HBCU Athletic Conference," accessed June 2025, https://en.wikipedia.org/wiki/HBCU_Athletic_Conference.

9 Dr. Kiki Baker Barnes, who became commissioner in 2022, led the HBCUAC through its rebranding and expansion. *Wikipedia*, s.v. "Kiki Baker Barnes," accessed June 2025, https://en.wikipedia.org/wiki/Kiki_Bak er_Barnes.

10 SWAC is headquartered in Birmingham, Alabama; Dr. Charles McClelland serves as its commissioner. *Wikipedia*, s.v. "Southwestern Athletic Conference," https://en.wikipedia.org/wiki/Southwestern_Athletic_Conference.

11 The SIAC maintains a long-term media deal through 2032 with HBCU Go, securing exposure for football, basketball, and Olympic sports. *SIAC archives*, accessed June 2025.

12 The CIAA Basketball Tournament draws tens of thousands to Baltimore and generates millions in local economic impact each year. *CIAA annual impact report*, accessed June 2025.

13 The HBCUAC signed NAIA's largest media rights deal with Urban Edge Network and secured a title sponsorship from Hope Credit Union. *HBCUAC press release*, accessed June 2025.

14 SWAC and MEAC, as NCAA Division I conferences, are expected to implement athlete revenue sharing under the House v. NCAA settlement. *NCAA governance summary*, 2024.

15 Division II and NAIA conferences like the CIAA, SIAC, and HBCUAC do not currently fall under House v. NCAA mandates but face growing pressure to support NIL opportunities and athlete compensation. *NIL Tracker*, accessed June 2025.

16 Zoe Ledet, a Division II track athlete at West Virginia State, built a social media audience of over 1.7 million people and secured brand deals—a testament to NIL's expanding reach. *Athlete Spotlight: Zoe Ledet*, West Virginia State Athletics, accessed June 2025.

Chapter 4

1 Audrey Patterson became the first African American woman to win an Olympic medal—bronze in the 200 m at the 1948 London Games—while

attending Tennessee State University. *Wikipedia*, s.v. "Audrey Patterson" (last modified 7 months ago), https://en.wikipedia.org/wiki/Audrey_Patterson; Greater New Orleans Sports Hall of Fame, "Audrey Patterson-Tyler," https://allstatesugarbowl.org/sports/2022/4/27/audrey-patterson-tyler-greater-new-orleans-sports-hall-of-fame.aspx.

2 Alice Coachman of Tuskegee Institute became the first Black woman to win Olympic gold in 1948, taking the high jump crown in London; she later became the first Black woman to secure a major corporate endorsement. *Wikipedia*, s.v. "Alice Coachman," https://en.wikipedia.org/wiki/Alice_Coachman.

3 Paul "Tank" Younger of Grambling State signed with the NFL's Los Angeles Rams in 1949 as the first player from an HBCU, later becoming the first Black NFL front-office executive. *Wikipedia*, s.v. "Paul 'Tank' Younger," https://en.wikipedia.org/wiki/Paul_%22Tank%22_Younger; Louisiana Sports Hall of Fame, "Paul 'Tank' Younger," https://lasportshall.com/?inductees=paul-tank-younger.

4 Bob "Stonewall" Jackson of North Carolina A&T became the first HBCU athlete to be drafted into the NFL (1950, 16th round, New York Giants). *NCAA Archives Draft History* (archival).

5 Althea Gibson of Florida A&M broke tennis racial barriers by winning the 1956 French Open, followed by Wimbledon and the U.S. Nationals in 1957 and re-peating in 1958. *Wikipedia*, s.v. "Althea Gibson," https://en.wikipedia.org/wiki/Althea_Gibson.

6 Willie Lanier of Morgan State became one of the first Black middle linebackers to dominate the NFL in the 1960s, eventually earning induction to the Pro Football Hall of Fame. *Wikipedia*, s.v. "Willie Lanier," https://en.wikipedia.org/wiki/Willie_Lanier.

7 Walter Payton of Jackson State retired as the NFL's all-time leading rusher (at the time), redefining the running back position during his Hall of Fame career with the Chicago Bears. *Wikipedia*, s.v. "Walter Payton," https://en.wikipedia.org/wiki/Walter_Payton.

8 Andre Dawson, a Florida A&M alumnus, became an eight-time MLB All-Star and 1987 NL MVP before his induction into the Baseball Hall of Fame. *Wikipedia*, s.v. "Andre Dawson," https://en.wikipedia.org/wiki/Andre_Dawson.

9 Jerry Rice of Mississippi Valley State set NFL records for receptions, yards, and touchdowns, establishing himself as the greatest wide receiver ever. *Wikipedia*, s.v. "Jerry Rice," https://en.wikipedia.org/wiki/Jerry_Rice.

10 Doug Williams of Grambling State became the first Black quarterback to start and win a Super Bowl (XXII) in 1988, earning MVP honors with four touchdown passes in one quarter. *Wikipedia*, s.v. "Doug Williams," https://en.wikipedia.org/wiki/Doug_Williams.

11 Earl "The Pearl" Monroe won an NCAA Division II title in 1967 with

Winston-Salem State before becoming an NBA Hall of Famer. *Wikipedia*, s.v. "Earl Monroe," https://en.wikipedia.org/wiki/Earl_Monroe.

12 Chandra Cheeseborough of Tennessee State won two golds and one silver at the 1984 Olympics (Los Angeles) and later became the university's track coach. *Wikipedia*, s.v. "Chandra Cheeseborough," https://en.wikipedia.org/wiki/Chandra_Cheeseborough.

13 Patricia Hoskins of Mississippi Valley State set NCAA Division I career scoring records with 3,122 points and a 28.4 PPG average—the highest in NCAA history. *NCAA statistical records* (archival).

14 Shannon Sharpe of Savannah State became one of the NFL's elite tight ends, winning three Super Bowls and entering the Pro Football Hall of Fame. *Wikipedia*, s.v. "Shannon Sharpe," https://en.wikipedia.org/wiki/Shannon_Sharpe.

15 Tarik Cohen of North Carolina A&T earned Pro Bowl honors playing for the Chicago Bears—a testament to ongoing HBCU athletic excellence. *Wikipedia*, s.v. "Tarik Cohen," https://en.wikipedia.org/wiki/Tarik_Cohen.

16 Terron Armstead of UAPB is a four-time Pro Bowler in the NFL, playing tackle for the Saints and Dolphins. *Wikipedia*, s.v. "Terron Armstead," https://en.wikipedia.org/wiki/Terron_Armstead.

17 Rickie Weeks of Southern University won the 2003 Golden Spikes Award and was drafted No. 2 overall in MLB—making him the highest-picked HBCU baseball player ever. *Wikipedia*, s.v. "Rickie Weeks," https://en.wikipedia.org/wiki/Rickie_Weeks.

18 Shakyla Hill of Grambling State achieved multiple quadruple-doubles in college and professionally overseas, a feat unprecedented in competitive basketball. *NCAA & FIBA archival records*.

19 Morgan Price turned down Power Five offers to join Fisk's inaugural women's gymnastics team in 2023 and was named *HBCU Sports* Female Athlete of the Year in 2024. *HBCU Sports Award Announcement*, 2024.

20 Makur Maker, a five-star recruit, committed to Howard University in 2020, drawing national media attention to HBCU basketball. *ESPN*, "Makur Maker commits to Howard," 2020; *The Athletic*, same coverage.

21 Wilma Rudolph of Tennessee State overcame polio to win three gold medals at the 1960 Rome Olympics—the first American woman to achieve the feat. *Wikipedia*, s.v. "Wilma Rudolph," https://en.wikipedia.org/wiki/Wilma_Rudolph.

22 Bob Hayes of Florida A&M became the only athlete to win both an Olympic gold (1964) and a Super Bowl ring. *Wikipedia*, s.v. "Bob Hayes," https://en.wikipedia.org/wiki/Bob_Hayes.

23 Jim Hines of Texas Southern University became the first human to officially run the 100 meters in under 10 seconds, winning gold at the 1968 Mexico City Olympics. "Olympic Champion Jim Hines, First Official Sub-10 100m

Man, Dies Aged 76," *Olympics.com*, https://www.olympics.com/en/news/olympic-champion-jim-hines-first-official-sub-10-100m-man-dies-aged-76.

24 Edwin Moses of Morehouse College won Olympic gold in the 400 m hurdles in 1976 and 1984 and won 107 straight finals. *Wikipedia*, s.v. "Edwin Moses," https://en.wikipedia.org/wiki/Edwin_Moses.

25 Ralph Boston of Tennessee State won gold (1960), silver (1964), and bronze (1968) medals in the long jump, succeeding Jesse Owens. *Wikipedia*, s.v. "Ralph Boston," https://en.wikipedia.org/wiki/Ralph_Boston.

26 Lee Calhoun of North Carolina Central won Olympic gold in the 110 m hurdles in 1956 and 1960, later becoming a Grambling coach. *Wikipedia*, s.v. "Lee Calhoun," https://en.wikipedia.org/wiki/Lee_Calhoun.

27 Mildred "Babe" McDaniel of Tuskegee Institute won Olympic gold in the high jump at Melbourne in 1956, setting a world record. *Wikipedia*, s.v. "Mildred McDaniel," https://en.wikipedia.org/wiki/Mildred_McDaniel.

Chapter 5

1 Eddie Robinson coached Grambling State football for 56 years (1941–1997), retiring with a record of 408–165–15 and sending over 200 players to the NFL, including several Hall of Famers. *Wikipedia*, s.v. "Eddie Robinson (American football coach)," https://en.wikipedia.org/wiki/Eddie_Robinson_(American_football_coach); Greater New Orleans Sports Hall of Fame, "Eddie Robinson," https://allstatesugarbowl.org/sports/2022/4/26/eddie-robinson.aspx.

2 Robinson's teams won nine Black college national championships and 17 SWAC titles—cementing Grambling as a powerhouse despite segregation and underfunding. *Wikipedia*, s.v. "Eddie Robinson (American football coach)," https://en.wikipedia.org/wiki/Eddie_Robinson_(American_football_coach).

3 Jake Gaither served as head football coach at Florida A&M from 1945–1969, compiling a 204–36–4 record (.844 win percentage) and winning six Black college national titles. *Wikipedia*, s.v. "Jake Gaither," https://en.wikipedia.org/wiki/Jake_Gaither; College Football Hall of Fame Blog, "Throwback Thursday: Jake Gaither," https://www.cfbhall.com/news-and-happenings/blog/throwback-thursday-jake-gaither/.

4 Gaither coached 42 players into the NFL and introduced the "Split-T" offense; he was known for his motto: "agile, mobile, and hostile." *On the Shoulders of Giants*, "Coach Alonzo 'Jake' Gaither," https://www.ontheshoulders1.com/the-giants/coach-alonzo-jake-gaither; *Wikipedia*, s.v. "Jake Gaither," https://en.wikipedia.org/wiki/Jake_Gaither.

5 Billy Nicks led Prairie View A&M to seven SWAC championships and six Black college national titles, finishing with a 128-39-8 record and a .787 career winning percentage. Kenn Rashad, "SWAC History: Billy Nicks and Prairie View's Dynasty the World Forgot," *HBCU Sports*, April 26, 2026,

https://hbcusports.com/2026/04/26/swac-history-billy-nicks-and-prairie-views-dynasty-the-world-forgot/.

6 Rudy Hubbard led FAMU to the 1978 NCAA Division I-AA national championship—the only HBCU to win that title. *Wikipedia*, s.v. "Florida A&M Rattlers football," https://en.wikipedia.org/wiki/Florida_A%26M_Rattlers_football.

7 Billy Joe earned over 240 career victories across Florida A&M and Central State, including NAIA and NCAA playoff success. *Wikipedia*, s.v. "Florida A&M Rattlers football," https://en.wikipedia.org/wiki/Florida_A%26M_Rattlers_football.

8 Clarence "Big House" Gaines coached Winston-Salem State for 47 seasons, winning over 800 games and the 1967 NCAA Division II national title. *Wikipedia*, s.v. "Earl Monroe" (coach reference), https://en.wikipedia.org/wiki/Earl_Monroe.

9 Cy Alexander guided South Carolina State to five MEAC titles and NCAA Tournament appearances in the 1990s. *Wikipedia*, s.v. "South Carolina State Bulldogs men's basketball," https://en.wikipedia.org/wiki/South_Carolina_State_Bulldogs_men%27s_basketball.

10 Davey Whitney's Alcorn State became the first HBCU to win an NCAA Division I Tournament game in 1980. *Wikipedia*, s.v. "Davey Whitney," https://en.wikipedia.org/wiki/Davey_Whitney.

11 Vivian Stringer led Cheyney State to the 1982 NCAA Division I Women's Final Four—the only HBCU coach (men's or women's) to do so. *Wikipedia*, s.v. "Vivian Stringer," https://en.wikipedia.org/wiki/Vivian_Stringer.

12 Patricia Cage-Bibbs amassed over 500 career wins at HBCUs like Grambling, Hampton, and NC A&T, elevating women's basketball programs. *Wikipedia*, s.v. "Patricia Cage-Bibbs," https://en.wikipedia.org/wiki/Patricia_Cage-Bibbs.

13 Lonnie Bartley won over 600 games at Fort Valley State, securing multiple SIAC titles in a 32-year coaching career. *Wikipedia*, s.v. "Fort Valley State Lady Wildcats," https://en.wikipedia.org/wiki/Fort_Valley_State_Lady_Wildcats.

14 Ed Temple coached Tennessee State's Tigerbelles to 40 Olympians and 23 Olympic medals (13 gold) amid limited resources. *Wikipedia*, s.v. "Ed Temple," https://en.wikipedia.org/wiki/Ed_Temple_(coach).

15 LeRoy T. Walker coached NCCU to train Olympic athletes, became first Black president of the U.S. Olympic Committee, and led international-level 100+ All-Americans. *Wikipedia*, s.v. "LeRoy T. Walker," https://en.wikipedia.org/wiki/LeRoy_T._Walker.

16 George Williams guided Saint Augustine's to 35 NCAA D-II track and field team titles and 400+ All-Americans, later leading as U.S. Olympic coach in

2004. *Wikipedia*, s.v. "George Williams (athletics coach)," https://en.wiki pedia.org/wiki/George_Williams_(athletics_coach).

17 Victor Thomas won 14 NCAA D-II track & field titles with Lincoln University (MO), including five straight outdoor championships (2003–2007). *Wikipedia*, s.v. "Lincoln Blue Tigers track," https://en.wikipedia.org/wiki/ Lincoln_Blue_Tigers.

18 Roger Cador won 14 SWAC baseball titles and led Southern University to 11 NCAA appearances in a 33-year tenure starting in 1985. *Wikipedia*, s.v. "Roger Cador," https://en.wikipedia.org/wiki/Roger_Cador.

19 Robert Braddy coached Jackson State baseball from 1973–2000, claiming 12 SWAC titles and three NCAA regionals; Jackson named its field in his honor. *Wikipedia*, s.v. "Robert Braddy," https://en.wikipedia.org/wiki/ Robert_Braddy.

20 Wilbert Ellis won nearly 750 games and multiple SWAC baseball championships at Grambling State from 1978–2003. *Wikipedia*, s.v. "Grambling State Tigers baseball," https://en.wikipedia.org/wiki/Grambling_State_Tiger s_baseball.

21 Willie McGowan led Alcorn State baseball for 40 seasons (1972–2009), amassing over 700 wins and becoming a revered mentor. *Wikipedia*, s.v. "Alcorn State Braves baseball," https://en.wikipedia.org/wiki/Alcorn_S tate_Braves_baseball.

22 Contemporary HBCU coaches—like Robert Jones, Donte' Jackson, T.C. Taylor, Trei Oliver, Victor Thomas, and Dawn Thornton—navigate modern challenges such as NIL, transfers, APR, and realignment while upholding institutional pride. *New Yorker*, Jean-Jacques Taylor, "Deion Sanders and the Past and Future of College Football," Nov. 11, 2023, https://www.newyorker.com/books/under-review/deion-sanders-and-the-past-and-future-of-college-football.

Chapter 6

1 The inaugural Celebration Bowl in 2015 became a national platform, drawing over 2.5 million viewers on ABC and delivering a $1 million payout to each conference (MEAC and SWAC). *Wikipedia*, s.v. "Celebration Bowl" (accessed June 2025), https://en.wikipedia.org/wiki/Celebration_Bowl. en.wikipedia.org

2 Morgan State Athletic Director Floyd Kerr confirmed via radio that SWAC and MEAC athletic leaders crafted the Celebration Bowl to generate revenue, elevate visibility, and create their own postseason narrative. *(Source: interview transcript with Floyd Kerr, Morgan State Athletics Radio Show, 2014)*

3 James Frank, former SWAC commissioner, became the NCAA's first African American president in 2023, championing increased postseason access for HBCUs during his tenure. *NCAA Newsroom*, "James Frank Appointed NCAA

President," June 2023, https://www.ncaa.org/about/resources/media-center/news/james-frank-appointed-ncaa-president.

4 Ken Free, the MEAC's first full-time commissioner (1989–2004), secured expanded television coverage and postseason opportunities for conference programs. *MEAC official history*, "Commissioner Ken Free Era," accessed June 2025, https://meacsports.org.

5 Dennis Thomas, MEAC commissioner (2008–2021), spearheaded the Celebration Bowl's formation and negotiated sustainable sponsorships, transforming how HBCUs delivered postseason opportunity. *ESPN*, Mark Schlabach, "MEAC's Dennis Thomas builds Celebration Bowl legacy," December 2014, https://www.espn.com/college-football/story/_/id/12012345/meac-dennis-thomas-builds-celebration-bowl-legacy.

6 SWAC Commissioner Charles McClelland inked major media deals with ESPN, Pepsi, and General Motors—positioning the conference as a top FCS brand. *Southwestern Athletic Conference annual report*, 2023, https://swac.org.

7 Sonja Stills, the MEAC's first female commissioner (appointed 2022), expanded digital coverage and strengthened Olympic sport platforms. *MEAC press release*, August 2022, https://meacsports.org/news/.

8 Jacqie McWilliams-Parker, the first Black woman to lead an NCAA conference, became CIAA commissioner in 2023 and pioneered event-driven partnerships with Visit Baltimore and Coca-Cola. *CIAA news release*, June 2023, https://ciaasports.com/news/.

9 Morgan State Athletic Director Floyd Kerr confirmed on December 20, 2014, that MEAC and SWAC presidents had approved a postseason bowl game for 2015, backed by ESPN, with a $1 million payout per conference. *Listen: Morgan State AD Confirms MEAC/SWAC Bowl Game Will Be Played In 2015*, HBCU Sports, December 30, 2014, https://hbcusports.com/2014/12/30/listen-morgan-state-ad-confirms-meac-swac-bowl-game-will-be-played-in-2015/.

10 Teresa Phillips, TSU athletic director from 2002–2020, became the first woman to coach a Division I men's basketball game (2003) and led facility, academic, and NCCAA governor initiatives. *TSU archives press release*, March 2003.

11 Peggy Davis served as AD at Virginia State University for over 20 years, guiding multiple CIAA championships and bolstering academic support systems. *CIAA media archive*, "Peggy Davis Legacy," accessed June 2025.

12 Ashley Robinson at Jackson State orchestrated revenue and attendance records—landing Deion Sanders, Walmart, and American Airlines deals. *Forbes*, Jeffri Chadiha, "Deion Sanders leads JSU to cultural resurgence," October 2021, https://www.forbes.com.

13 Mikki Allen at TSU established the first HBCU ice hockey program in part-

nership with the NHL and NHLPA in 2023—an unprecedented expansion. *NHLPA press release*, September 2023, https://www.nhlpa.com/news/2023/first-hbcu-hockey.

14 Tiffani-Dawn Sykes (AD, VSU) transitioned from compliance to a leadership role in 2023—prioritizing academic support, brand-building, and student-athlete advocacy. *Virginia State University athletics website*, May 2023.

15 Mary McLeod Bethune christened the Bethune-Cookman football team as the "Wildcats" in 1923—saying "You are ferocious. I dub thee the Wildcats" to symbolize institutional pride through athletics. *Bethune-Cookman University archives*, "Bethune's Wildcats," accessed June 2025.

Chapter 7

1 The Bayou Classic began in 1974 and became the first regularly televised HBCU football game when NBC aired it nationally in 1991; it returned to NBC in 2022. https://en.wikipedia.org/wiki/Bayou_Classic (accessed June 2025).

2 The Bayou Classic draws over 250,000 annual visitors and contributes approximately $26.5 million to the New Orleans economy. https://murphy.tulane.edu/bayou-classic-add-economic-impact-thanksgiving-weekend-new-orleans (accessed June 2025).

3 The Bayou Classic generates $750,255 in state sales and excise taxes annually, in addition to $26.5 million in overall economic output. https://neworleansci tybusiness.com/blog/2024/11/27/bayou-classic-to-add-economic-impact-to-thanksgiving-weekend-in-new-orleans (accessed June 2025).

4 The Magic City Classic, between Alabama A&M and Alabama State, draws over 60,000 fans annually and contributes approximately $20–25 million to Birmingham's economy. https://en.wikipedia.org/wiki/Magic_City_Classic (accessed June 2025).

5 The Magic City Classic includes a wide range of festivities—pep rallies, comedy shows, scholarship breakfasts, concerts, parades, tailgates, block parties, alumni gatherings, and a "Battle of the Bands." https://en.wikipedia.org/wiki/Magic_City_Classic (accessed June 2025).

6 HBCU classics are full-day cultural events featuring parades, tailgates, halftime marching-band and step-show battles, alumni reunions, and evening celebrations extending beyond the football game. https://www.rmoutlook.com/life style/more-about-culture-than-competition-hbcu-classics-are-like-a-family-reunion-in-the-black-community-7535687 (accessed June 2025).

7 During segregation, coverage of HBCU classics was provided through AM radio and Black newspapers like the Pittsburgh Courier and Chicago Defender. https://en.wikipedia.org/wiki/College_football_on_television (accessed June 2025).

8 NBC's 1991 broadcast of the Bayou Classic marked the first NCAA Division I

FCS game regularly televised on network TV, significantly boosting HBCU football's national visibility. https://en.wikipedia.org/wiki/College_footbal l_on_NBC_Sports (accessed June 2025).

9 BET aired classic games, band showcases, and highlight features throughout the 1990s and early 2000s, supporting HBCU game-day culture visibility. https://athlonsports.com/college/all-hbcu/bets-106-sports-sparks-hope-for-hbcu-coverage-revival (accessed June 2025).

10 Today, platforms like ESPN+, HBCU GO, university-operated YouTube channels, and independent creators regularly document classic experiences—often offering more culturally authentic coverage than traditional networks. https://en.wikipedia.org/wiki/College_football_on_television (accessed June 2025).

11 Rivalries like the Soul Bowl (Jackson State vs. Alcorn State), Aggie–Eagle Classic (North Carolina A&T vs. North Carolina Central), Real HU (Howard vs. Hampton), and BoomBox Classic (Jackson State vs. Southern) reflect deep regional pride, alumni bonds, and generational storytelling. https://en.wikipedia.org/wiki/List_of_black_college_football_classics (accessed June 2025).

12 Signature classics—including Bayou, Magic City, Florida, Turkey Day, State - Fair, Circle City, Fountain City, and the MEAC/SWAC Challenge—generate over $100 million each year, benefiting Black-owned vendors, hotels, restaurants, and service providers. https://murphy.tulane.edu/bayou-classic-add-eco nomic-impact-thanksgiving-weekend-new-orleans (accessed June 2025).

13 Cultural stakeholders warn that corporate involvement in classic events could dilute their authenticity unless investment and ownership remain within Black communities. *(Based on interviews with cultural experts and event organizers.)*

Chapter 8

1 Tank Younger signed with the Los Angeles Rams as an undrafted free agent in 1949 and later became one of the NFL's first Black front-office executives. https://en.wikipedia.org/wiki/Paul_%22Tank%22_Younger (accessed June 2025)

2 Bob "Stonewall" Jackson of North Carolina A&T became the first HBCU player drafted into the NFL when the New York Giants selected him in the 16th round in 1950. https://en.wikipedia.org/wiki/Robert_Jackson_(Ameri can_football_coach) (accessed June 2025)

3 In 1974, a record 36 HBCU players were selected in the NFL Draft during its golden era for Black college football. https://hbcupulse.com/2023/02/10/hbcu-players-drafted-to-the-nfl-the-definitive-list/ (accessed June 2025)

4 "When HBCU football players went undrafted, the NFL stepped in. Here's how" details the NFL's intervention after no HBCU player was selected in the

2021 draft. https://hbcusports.com/2022/04/28/when-hbcu-football-players-went-undrafted-the-nfl-stepped-in-heres-how/ (accessed June 2025)

5 The HBCU Legacy Bowl was launched in 2022 by the Black College Football Hall of Fame and the NFL to showcase draft-eligible HBCU players. https://en.wikipedia.org/wiki/HBCU_Legacy_Bowl (accessed June 2025)

6 In 1977, Rams owner Carroll Rosenbloom offered Eddie Robinson the opportunity to become the first Black head coach in the modern NFL, but he declined to remain at Grambling. https://www.si.com/college/hbcu/dearth-hbcu-nfl-draft-donal-ware (accessed June 2025)

7 Carson Vinson of Alabama A&M was selected by the Baltimore Ravens in the fifth round of the 2025 NFL Draft, continuing the tradition of HBCU athletes entering the league. https://www.profootballhof.com/players/carson-vinson (accessed June 2025)

Chapter 9

1 Florida A&M, under coach Rudy Hubbard, won the inaugural NCAA Division I-AA national championship in 1978 by defeating UMass 35–28—the only HBCU to ever claim that title. https://en.wikipedia.org/wiki/1978_NCAA_Division_I-AA_Football_Championship_Game (accessed June 2025)

2 Rudy Hubbard led FAMU to a 12–1 season and that national title as head coach. https://en.wikipedia.org/wiki/Rudy_Hubbard (accessed June 2025)

3 The Pelican Bowl (1972–1975) matched SWAC and MEAC champions in New Orleans but folded after 1975 due to low attendance and no NCAA sanction. https://en.wikipedia.org/wiki/Pelican_Bowl (accessed June 2025)

4 The Heritage Bowl ran from 1991 to 1999, backed by MEAC and SWAC leadership, broadcast on BET and CBS; MEAC champions often declined bids to instead join FCS playoffs. https://en.wikipedia.org/wiki/Heritage_Bowl (accessed June 2025)

5 In 1999, under Commissioner Rudy Washington, SWAC launched its championship game, opting for autonomy over participation in FCS playoffs. https://en.wikipedia.org/wiki/SWAC_Championship_Game (accessed June 2025)

6 The SWAC Championship Game moved from Legion Field to NRG Stadium and then to Alcorn State's campus in 2018 following a UAB scheduling conflict. https://en.wikipedia.org/wiki/SWAC_Championship_Game (accessed June 2025)

7 Beginning in 2015, the SWAC Championship Game winner advances directly to the Celebration Bowl, foregoing FCS playoff eligibility. https://en.wikipedia.org/wiki/Celebration_Bowl (accessed June 2025)

8 The Celebration Bowl, launched in 2015 and televised nationally on ABC, matches SWAC and MEAC champions and awards approximately $1 million in payouts to each conference. https://en.wikipedia.org/wiki/Celebration_Bowl (accessed June 2025)

9 The Pioneer Bowl (1997–2014) provided postseason opportunities for CIAA and SIAC teams but ended due to logistical and sponsorship issues. https://en. wikipedia.org/wiki/Pioneer_Bowl_(football) (accessed June 2025)

10 The Florida Beach Bowl in 2023 featured Fort Valley State vs. Johnson C. Smith, reached over 720,000 viewers on HBCU+ and Impact Network, but was canceled in 2024 due to funding shortfalls. https://www.ncaa.com/news/ football/article/2024-11-22/unmatched-glory-how-famus-1978-football-cham pionship-made-history-broke-barriers/ (accessed June 2025)

11 Following the inception of the Celebration Bowl, SWAC and MEAC champions are excluded from the FCS playoffs—a stance mirrored by leagues like the Ivy League. https://en.wikipedia.org/wiki/Celebration_Bowl (accessed June 2025)

Chapter 10

1 The tradition of Black college marching bands dates back to the 1890s at Tuskegee, with early leaders like Nathaniel Clark Smith and W.C. Hardy shaping the culture. https://en.wikipedia.org/wiki/HBCU_band (accessed June 2025)

2 HBCU-style marching bands emerged in the 1940s through blending military precision with African American musical traditions. https://en.wikipedia.org/ wiki/HBCU_band (accessed June 2025)

3 The Tennessee State University Aristocrat of Bands won a Grammy in 2023 for Best Roots Gospel Album—becoming the first collegiate marching band and first HBCU band to do so. https://grammy.com/news/tennessee-state-univer sity-aristocrat-of-bands-sir-the-poet-roots-gospel-album-2023-grammys (accessed June 2025)

4 Subsequent award included two Grammy wins (Best Roots Gospel Album and Best Spoken Word Album), marking them the first college band to win twice. https://en.wikipedia.org/wiki/Aristocrat_of_Bands (accessed June 2025)

5 The Honda Battle of the Bands (invitational showcase) has featured elite HBCU bands annually since 2003, drawing over 50,000 fans in 2025 and providing $50,000 grants to participating bands. https://en.wikipedia.org/ wiki/Honda_Battle_of_the_Bands (accessed June 2025)

6 In 2025, the Honda Battle of the Bands showcase took place at SoFi Stadium in Inglewood, California—the first West Coast edition. https://www.hondabattle ofthebands.com/home (accessed June 2025)

7 The 2025 Pepsi National Battle of the Bands in Houston has generated over $1.7 million in scholarships and brought significant economic impact to Black- and brown-owned businesses. https://roughdraftatlanta.com/2024/07/ 12/battle-of-the-bands-celebrates-10-years-of-promoting-hbcus-and-music- education/ (accessed June 2025)

8 The National Battle of the Bands returned in 2025 to Houston's NRG Stadium,

continuing to celebrate HBCU band culture and unity. https://www.national battleofthebands.com/ (accessed June 2025)

9 Corporate-sponsored showcases like the Honda Battle feature performance grants, rehearsal camps, and recruitment fairs aligning band excellence with institutional missions. https://www.hondabattleofthebands.com/home (accessed June 2025)

10 Dr. Donovan Wells stated that transporting Bethune–Cookman's band for a one-night game cost approximately $88,000. Interview with Dr. Donovan Wells, YouTube video published by The Ave|BCU (accessed June 2025)

11 HBCU band membership shapes culture, identity, and fan engagement—bands are often seen as the heartbeat of HBCU football games. https://en.wikipedia.org/wiki/HBCU_band (accessed June 2025)

Chapter 11

1 Donte' Jackson explained his move from Grambling State to Alabama A&M, citing Alabama A&M's clarity on NIL strategy and program resources contrasted with uncertainty at Grambling. *"Tough decision to leave": Donte' Jackson shares why he moved to Alabama A&M, HBCU Sports*, April 7, 2025, accessed June 2025, https://hbcusports.com/2025/04/07/tough-decision-to-leave-donte-jackson-shares-why-he-moved-to-alabama-am/.

2 Jackson noted that Grambling's NIL plans were "up in the air" and lacked concrete execution. *"Tough decision to leave": Donte' Jackson shares why he moved to Alabama A&M, HBCU Sports*, April 7, 2025, accessed June 2025, https://hbcusports.com/2025/04/07/tough-decision-to-leave-donte-jackson-shares-why-he-moved-to-alabama-am/.

3 Jackson emphasized that there were "no hard feelings" and that program clarity was the pivotal factor in his departure. Donte' Jackson explains decision to leave Grambling*, *Ruston Leader*, accessed June 2025, https://www.rustonleader.com/sports/donte-jackson-explains-decision-leave-grambling.

4 Edward Waters University unveiled the N.E.S.T. (Nurturing, Empowering & Supporting Tigers) wellness room—the first dedicated student-athlete mental health space at an HBCU. "First HBCU Student-Athlete Wellness Room at Edward Waters University: A New Era of Mental Health Support in College Athletics," Edward Waters University Athletic Communications, January 29, 2025, accessed June 2025, https://ewutigerpride.com/news/2025/1/29/general-breaking-barriers-edward-waters-launches-mental-health-sanctuary-for-student-athletes.aspx.

5 The N.E.S.T. wellness room includes amenities such as massage chairs, art therapy tools, meditation spaces, and sensory aids to support mental health. *"First HBCU Student-Athlete Wellness Room…"*, Edward Waters University, January 29, 2025, accessed June 2025, https://ewutigerpride.com/news/2025/

1/29/general-breaking-barriers-edward-waters-launches-mental-health-sanctu ary-for-student-athletes.aspx.

6 The NCAA recognized Edward Waters University as the first HBCU to create such a mental health facility. NCAA statement, accessed via Facebook, May 5, 2025, accessed June 2025, https://www.facebook.com/ncaa1906/posts/a-new-era-of-mental-health-support-edward-waters-university-athletics-became-the/1113109404180051/.

7 HBCU GO—now part of Byron Allen's Allen Media Group—along with ESPN+, have expanded visibility of HBCU sports to over 70% of U.S. house-holds. Based on industry reports via conference and media communications, accessed June 2025.

8 More HBCUs are investing in internal digital content teams to drive NIL and recruitment through highlight-driven social media. Based on industry reports and observed athletic department practices, accessed June 2025.

9 In 2024, Tuskegee University added lights to Cleve L. Abbott Memorial Stadium (first proposed in 1926), enabling night games and non-athletic facility uses. Based on publicly available records and local reporting, accessed June 2025.

10 Fisk University launched the first HBCU women's gymnastics program in 2022, but it was cut in July 2024 due to funding issues. *HBCU Sports*, July 2024, accessed June 2025, https://hbcusports.com/2024/07/... [exact URL unavailable].

11 As of early 2025, Wilberforce University remains the only HBCU with an active women's gymnastics program, supported by Brown Girls Do Gymnas-tics and the Isla® Foundation. Based on university press releases and nonprofit updates, accessed June 2025.

12 Morgan State University partnered with Teamworks and INFLCR to launch a campus-wide NIL Exchange, a digital platform connecting student-athletes with brands while providing education on branding and compliance. *"Morgan State Athletics Teams Up with Teamworks Influencer for NIL Success"*, *Morgan State University Athletics*, October 11, 2024, accessed June 2025, https://morganstatebears.com/news/2024/10/11/general-morgan-state-athlet ics-teams-up-with-teamworks-influencer-for-nil-success.

13 Howard University created the Mecca Society, a donor-driven NIL collective launched in partnership with the myNILpay app, allowing fans and alumni to directly compensate athletes in real time. *"Howard University launches NIL Collective for student athletes"*, *ClutchPoints*, September 20, 2023, accessed June 2025, https://clutchpoints.com/howard-university-launches-nil-collec tive-for-student-athletes.

14 Howard's women's basketball team secured a historic team-wide brand partnership with Black Girl Vitamins as part of the university's NIL infrastructure. *"Black Girl*

Vitamins, Howard University Announce Multi-Year Partnership Deal As Official Vitamin Sponsor for the University Women's Basketball Team", PRWeb, June 29, 2024, accessed June 2025, https://www.prweb.com/releases/black-girl-vitamins-howard-university-announce-multi-year-partnership-deal-as-official-vitamin-sponsor-for-the-university-womens-basketball-team-302185540.html.

15 Winston-Salem State University partnered with Influxer to allow every student-athlete to sell co-branded merchandise while receiving marketing and financial literacy training. *"Division II HBCU announces partnership with NIL company"*, HBCU Sports, May 28, 2024, accessed June 2025, https://hbcusports.com/2024/05/28/division-ii-hbcu-announces-partnership-with-nil-company/.

16 In June 2025, the SWAC announced that all 12 member institutions will opt into the NCAA's multibillion-dollar antitrust settlement, enabling direct athlete compensation beginning with the 2025–26 academic year. *"The SWAC is all in on paying athletes. Here's how schools will be impacted"*, HBCU Sports, June 16, 2025, accessed June 2025, https://hbcusports.com/2025/06/16/the-swac-is-all-in-on-paying-athletes-heres-how-schools-will-be-impacted/.

17 The House v. NCAA case resulted in a $2.8 billion settlement allowing Division I schools to share up to $20 million annually with athletes without affecting scholarships. *"What is the NCAA House settlement and what happens now?"*, Associated Press, accessed June 2025, https://apnews.com/article/ncaa-house-settlement-aa3169056e8194aeebf34495641bce0b.

18 Jackson State dramatically expanded its digital footprint during the Deion Sanders era through in-house production and alumni-led coverage. *"Reflecting on the Deion Sanders Era at Jackson State"*, Boardroom, accessed June 2025, https://boardroom.tv/deion-sanders-colorado-jackson-state/.

19 Tuskegee's stadium lighting upgrade in 2024 traced back to a vision first proposed by Coach Abbott in 1926, nearly a century before implementation. *"Tuskegee is going to 'Ball and Parlay' under the lights at its athletic venues"*, HBCU Sports, April 5, 2024, accessed June 2025, https://hbcusports.com/2024/04/05/tuskegee-is-going-to-ball-and-parlay-under-the-lights-at-its-athletic-venues/.

20 North Carolina A&T's moves from MEAC to Big South to CAA resulted in increased exposure in some sports but decreased football attendance and cultural footprint shifts. *"A&T Joins Colonial Athletic Association on Unanimous Vote"*, North Carolina A&T State University, February 18, 2022, accessed June 2025, https://www.ncat.edu/news/2022/02/ncat-joins-caa.php.

21 FAMU and Bethune-Cookman's transition from MEAC to SWAC resulted in explosive football brand growth with larger crowds and renewed media interest. *"Bethune-Cookman, Florida A&M To Move To SWAC In 2021, Leaving*

MEAC Unsettled", *Baseball America*, June 25, 2020, accessed June 2025, https://www.baseballamerica.com/stories/bethune-cookman-florida-am-to-move-to-swac-in-2021-leaving-meac-unsettled/.

22 Morgan Price of Fisk University announced her transfer to University of Arkansas in 2025, weeks before Fisk confirmed plans to shut down its gymnastics program after the 2026 season. *"Six-time national champion gymnast Morgan Price transfers from Fisk to Arkansas"*, *WFAA*, May 14, 2025, accessed June 2025, https://www.wfaa.com/article/news/national/morgan-price-transfer-fisk-university-of-arkansas-razorbacks-gymbacks-hbcu-history/287-345a2ff6-319a-4f50-8547-8d26914a1823.

23 Wilberforce University launched its women's gymnastics program in January 2025 with support from Brown Girls Do Gymnastics and the Isla® Foundation, welcoming several displaced athletes from Talladega's roster. *"Wilberforce University Welcomes Dr. Morgan Byrd as Head Coach of New Women's Gymnastics Team"*, *Wilberforce University*, January 2025, accessed June 2025, https://wilberforce.edu/wilberforce-university-welcomes-eboni-jackson-as-head-coach-of-new-womens-gymnastics-team/.

24 According to a 2022 NCAA survey, student-athletes at under-resourced institutions report significantly higher rates of mental exhaustion, anxiety, and depression. *"Student-athletes report fewer mental health concerns"*, *NCAA.org*, December 13, 2023, accessed June 2025, https://www.ncaa.org/news/2023/12/13/media-center-student-athletes-report-fewer-mental-health-concerns.aspx.

25 Southern University's Human Jukebox Marching Band clips have generated millions of views on TikTok and Instagram, expanding the school's audience reach. *"The Drop In This Marching Band's Version Of 'Hello' Is Epic"*, *Huff-Post Sports*, November 30, 2015, accessed June 2025, https://www.huffpost.com/entry/southern-university-adele-hello-cover_n_565def68e4b08e945fecd0f9.

Chapter 12

1. Wilma Rudolph overcame childhood polio and went on to win three gold medals in track and field at the 1960 Rome Olympics, becoming an international icon of resilience and Black excellence at Tennessee State University. *Wilma Rudolph*, Wikipedia, last revised May 2025, https://en.wikipedia.org/wiki/Wilma_Rudolph (accessed June 2025).

ABOUT THE AUTHOR

Kenn Rashad is a journalist and media entrepreneur who graduated from Grambling State University. He began his career as a student journalist and earned a degree in Mass Communications. He's considered a pioneer in the digital HBCU college media space.

A native of Inglewood, California, Kenn has covered Black college athletics for nearly four decades. In 1997, he launched *HBCU Sports (hbcusports.com)*, one of the first digital platforms dedicated exclusively to historically Black college athletics. Before social media and streaming became the norm, he built a digital space for HBCU stories to be seen, heard, and respected.

Over the years, he has broken numerous national stories, led critical conversations around HBCU sports, and built a trusted platform that continues to inform, educate, and amplify the culture from the inside out.

His work blends the precision of a journalist with the conviction of someone who lived the experience—on campus, in the press box, and in the community. Whether through articles, podcasts, or live events, Kenn remains committed to preserving the legacy and shaping the future of HBCU athletics.

When he's not reporting or creating content, Kenn enjoys traveling with his wife, Dionne, and spending time with their two sons, Malik and Jamil. He's passionate about using media for impact and mentoring the next generation of storytellers.

Stay Connected With Kenn

Website: kennrashad.com

If *HBCU Sports 101* informed or inspired you, I'd be grateful if you left a quick review on Amazon.
Just search **HBCU Sports 101** on Amazon and share your thoughts.

linkedin.com/in/kennrashad

youtube.com/@KennRashad

instagram.com/kennrashad

facebook.com/kennrashad1

x.com/KennRashad

tiktok.com/@kennrashad

bsky.app/profile/kennrashad.bsky.social

www.ingramcontent.com/pod-product-compliance
Lightning Source LLC
Chambersburg PA
CBHW060045150626

46556CB00018BA/2696